THE OECD GUIDELINES FOR MULTINATIONAL ENTERPRISES

ORGANISATION FOR ECONOMIC CO-OPERATION AND DEVELOPMENT

ORGANISATION FOR ECONOMIC CO-OPERATION AND DEVELOPMENT

Pursuant to Article 1 of the Convention signed in Paris on 14th December 1960, and which came into force on 30th September 1961, the Organisation for Economic Co-operation and Development (OECD) shall promote policies designed:

— to achieve the highest sustainable economic growth and employment and a rising standard of living in Member countries, while maintaining financial stability, and thus to contribute to the development of the world economy;

— to contribute to sound economic expansion in Member as well as non-member countries in the process of economic development; and

— to contribute to the expansion of world trade on a multilateral, non-discriminatory basis in accordance with international obligations.

The original Member countries of the OECD are Austria, Belgium, Canada, Denmark, France, Germany, Greece, Iceland, Ireland, Italy, Luxembourg, the Netherlands, Norway, Portugal, Spain, Sweden, Switzerland, Turkey, the United Kingdom and the United States. The following countries became Members subsequently through accession at the dates indicated hereafter: Japan (28th April 1964), Finland (28th January 1969), Australia (7th June 1971) and New Zealand (29th May 1973). The Commission of the European Communities takes part in the work of the OECD (Article 13 of the OECD Convention).

Publié en français sous le titre :

LES PRINCIPES DIRECTEURS DE L'OCDE
A L'INTENTION DES ENTREPRISES MULTINATIONALES

9264141094

PREFACE

The OECD Guidelines for Multinational Enterprises are an essential component of the 1976 Declaration on International Investment and Multinational Enterprises. The Guidelines are recommendations jointly addressed by the OECD governments to multinational enterprises operating in their territories. Setting voluntary standards of behaviour, they provide guidance to multinational enterprises and help to ensure that their operations are in harmony with the policies of the countries in which they operate.

The Guidelines seek to encourage the positive contributions which multinational enterprises can make to economic and social progress by helping to resolve difficulties to which their operations may give rise. This applies to the activities of multinational enterprises in OECD Member countries and, indeed, throughout the world.

This report explains the nature and scope of the Guidelines. Its purpose is to make the Guidelines better known and to contribute to their effective implementation.

TABLE OF CONTENTS

Chapter I

INTRODUCTION

The OECD Guidelines for Multinational Enterprises (MNEs) are recommendations to enterprises from OECD governments to help ensure that multinational businesses operate in harmony with the policies of the countries where they operate. These voluntary standards cover the full range of MNEs' operations: general policies, information disclosure, competition, financing, taxation, employment and industrial relations, environment, and science and technology.

Since the Guidelines' adoption in 1976, the OECD has given attention to making them known and has established follow-up procedures to assist in their implementation. This includes the establishment of Contact Points in Member countries to deal with Guidelines issues, regular OECD reviews of the Guidelines, periodic consultations with the business and industry and trade union advisory committees, and promotional activities.

Major reviews in 1979, 1982, 1984, and 1991 contain clarifications, comments and explanations on the Guidelines[1]. There have been very few amendments to the original Guidelines, as their effective application depends in part on their stability. Multinational companies, through the Business and Industry Advisory Committee (BIAC), and employees, through the Trade Union Advisory Committee (TUAC), support the Guidelines as a balanced and fair approach to addressing questions that may arise from MNE operations. The Guidelines should, therefore, continue to help improve understanding between business, governments and labour. In this way, they complement national legislation and reinforce MNEs' contributions to economic and social progress in host and home countries.

The Guidelines enjoy the full support of the OECD's 24 Member countries, where most MNEs are headquartered and where a substantial part of their operations are located. OECD Members have also declared their support for extending international co-operation in this field to all countries. The Guidelines have been published in some fifteen different languages[2] and are an important part of the dialogue with non-Member countries, especially those in Asia, Latin

America and Central and Eastern Europe with which OECD has developed closer ties.

Important developments have occurred since the OECD Guidelines for Multinational Enterprises were agreed in 1976. In general, there is today a wider acceptance of foreign direct investment and multinational enterprises, and competition for FDI is on the rise[3]. OECD countries, as well as many countries outside the OECD, are trying to attract a greater share of a limited pool of investment capital. This includes not only the countries of Central and Eastern Europe and the former Soviet Union, where new regulatory regimes are being developed to attract investment, but also developing countries in Asia, Africa and Latin America, which are disillusioned with past experience in restricting foreign investment and are now actively seeking more MNE involvement. New players have also emerged to which the Guidelines could apply, but who may not know about them, such as companies which before were not investing much abroad but today are becoming important international investors. These enterprises should find that the Guidelines provide helpful internationally accepted standards for their foreign operations.

These changes suggest more efforts are needed to increase awareness of the Guidelines, especially given the complexity and rapidity of business decisions in today's competitive commercial environment, the increasing number of multinational enterprises and the potential for conflict that could accompany these developments. Problems that could arise in regard to MNE operations can neither always be anticipated nor solved by the Guidelines, but companies that know and apply the Guidelines are less likely to encounter difficulties, and the Guidelines process makes it possible for business, governments and labour to address problems and seek understandings.

This booklet is part of the effort to make the Guidelines better known. It is designed as a general introduction and guide to all who may be interested in the Guidelines. Chapter II tells how the Guidelines came to be and describes their main features and how they fit with other OECD instruments on foreign direct investment. Chapter III explains how the Guidelines work, including the role of the National Contact Points, the social partners, and the OECD bodies involved in Guidelines activities. Chapter IV provides a commentary on how certain provisions of the Guidelines should be understood as a result of clarifications by the OECD Committee on International Investment and Multinational Enterprises ("CIME"). This chapter, however, does not modify the authoritative texts, which are found in the verbatim language of the Guidelines and the relevant CIME decisions referred to in footnotes to the text. The concluding Chapter V sums up experience with the Guidelines and briefly examines their role in the years ahead. The full text of the Guidelines themselves and the follow-up procedures are reproduced in Annexes 1 and 2, respectively. The list of National Contact Points appears in Annex 3.

Notes

1. See the Review reports: *International Investment and Multinational Enterprises: Review of the 1976 Declaration and Decisions* (OECD Paris, 1979); *Mid-Term Report on the 1976 Declaration and Decisions* (OECD Paris, 1982); *1984 Review of the 1976 Declaration and Decisions* (OECD Paris, 1984); *The OECD Declaration and Decisions on International Investment and Multinational Enterprises, 1991 Review* (OECD Paris, 1992).

2. The Guidelines are issued by OECD in English and French, and have been translated by the national authorities of Member countries into German, Japanese, Norwegian, Portuguese, Spanish and Swedish. The Guidelines are also available in the following languages of non-Member countries: Chinese (Cantonese), Hungarian, Polish, Russian, Czech and Slovak.

3. For more information on international direct investment trends and policies, see *International Direct Investment: Policies and Trends in the 1980s* (OECD Paris, 1992).

Chapter II

NATURE AND SCOPE OF THE GUIDELINES

1. Origins

The OECD Guidelines for Multinational Enterprises were designed to encourage the positive contribution which MNEs can make to economic and social progress and to help minimise and resolve the difficulties to which their operations may give rise. They were also intended to contribute to improving the foreign investment climate. The Guidelines were thus a response to the opportunities and challenges that MNEs represent.

While the Guidelines were the first internationally agreed framework for co-operation in the field of multinational enterprises, they were not the only effort. Proposals for a United Nations Code of Conduct on Transnational Corporations were not accepted, but UN Principles and Rules on Restrictive Business Practices were agreed. The International Labour Organisation (ILO) adopted in 1977 the Tripartite Declaration of Principles concerning Multinational Enterprises and Social Policy, a non-binding declaration addressed to governments, business and labour in the ILO's 159 member States. The Tripartite Declaration sets out principles in the fields of employment, training, working conditions, and industrial relations, while the OECD Guidelines cover all major aspects of corporate behaviour. Wherever the ILO Tripartite Declaration refers to the behaviour expected from enterprises, they parallel the OECD Guidelines and do not conflict with them.

When the Guidelines were adopted in 1976, multinational enterprises (MNEs) had come to play an important part in the economies of Member countries and in international economic relations. Through international direct investment, MNEs were known to bring substantial benefits to home and host countries by contributing to an efficient use of capital, technology and human resources between countries. MNEs could thus fulfil an important role in promoting economic and social welfare. At the same time, the ability of MNEs to organise their operations beyond the national framework led to concerns about possible conflicts with national policies and concentrations of economic power. The difficulty of clearly perceiving MNEs' sometimes complex structures, operations and policies sometimes gave rise to concern.

Attitudes towards MNEs are different today. They are widely accepted as an integral part of the international economy and the agent for beneficial flows of capital and diffusion of technology. As governments have gained experience with MNEs they have become more confident with them. MNEs, too, have become more attuned to the needs and sensitivities of governments and mutual confidence between business, government and labour has gradually built up. Nonetheless, even as most countries try to attract the benefits of direct investment, the Guidelines remain an important element in international economic co-operation.

2. Main features

The Guidelines have several distinguishing features that helped them gain acceptance and continue to ensure they are supported. First, observance of the Guidelines is voluntary and not legally enforceable. Their voluntary nature, however, does not imply less commitment by OECD Governments to encourage their observance. The active system under which the Guidelines are promoted and implemented, discussed in Chapter III, attests to the importance Members give the Guidelines.

Also, the Guidelines' basic approach is moderate. The assumption is not that enterprises need to be "controlled" but that internationally agreed guidelines can help prevent misunderstandings and build an atmosphere of mutual confidence and predictability between business, labour and governments. A continuing, pragmatic and balanced approach has characterised the Guidelines process and helped make them work.

Finally, the Guidelines are part of a package. They are one part of the OECD Declaration on International Investment and Multinational Enterprises, a broad political commitment adopted by the OECD Governments in 1976 to facilitate direct investment among OECD Members[1]. The other parts of the Declaration deal with three related elements:

-- The *National Treatment instrument* (NTI) sets out Member countries' commitments to treat foreign-controlled enterprises operating in their territories no less favourably than domestic enterprises in like situations;

-- An instrument on *International Investment Incentives and Disincentives* provides for efforts among Member countries to improve co-operation on measures affecting international direct investment;

-- An instrument on *Conflicting Requirements* calls on Member countries to avoid or minimise conflicting requirements imposed on multinational enterprises by governments of different countries.

In addition, the OECD has a long-standing instrument for treating new foreign investment, i.e. establishment by non-residents. The OECD Code of Liberalisation of Capital Movements, in force since the Organisation's founding in 1961, calls for progressive, nondiscriminatory liberalisation of international capital movements. Since 1984, the Code's liberalisation obligations have been applied to inward direct investment and establishment by investors in OECD Member countries[2].

The Capital Movements Code, the NTI, and the Guidelines form a comprehensive, interlinked and balanced approach for governments' treatment of foreign direct investment and for enterprises' activities in OECD countries. The OECD instruments on international investment and multinational enterprises are the main means by which OECD Members work towards a liberal regime for foreign direct investment, while at the same time ensuring MNEs operate in harmony with the countries where they are located.

3. Coverage

The Guidelines cover the range of MNE activities. They begin with an introduction and are followed by chapters on: General Policies, Disclosure of Information, Competition, Financing, Taxation, Employment and Industrial Relations, Environmental Protection, and Science and Technology. This section gives an indication of important themes that run through the Guidelines. It does not attempt to detail each chapter's provisions: the Guidelines themselves should be consulted for this. The clarification of certain provisions is discussed in Chapter IV.

The Guidelines' introductory paragraphs explain their purpose, nature and scope, making clear that they are addressed to MNEs and all their entities, and that these entities should co-operate with each other to facilitate observance of the Guidelines. The introduction also makes clear that the Guidelines do not introduce different treatment between MNEs and domestic enterprises and that the same expectations of good conduct apply equally to both. The General Policies chapter gives guidance of a general nature, saying enterprises should take Member countries' general policy objectives fully into account, co-operate with local community and business interests, and refrain from bribery and improper political activities.

Making information on the enterprise available -- to the public, government officials and workers -- is an important Guidelines theme. For the public, this involves having information on the structure, activities and policies of the enterprise as a whole. For governments, this means access to information to

13

ensure compliance with policies and regulations on taxes, competition and environmental standards. For employees, this involves having information provided to their representatives for purposes such as meaningful negotiations on conditions of employment, or information to enable them to obtain a true and fair view of the performance of an entity or, where appropriate, the enterprise as a whole.

A chapter of the Guidelines addresses employment and industrial relations, where enterprises are encouraged to respect employees' rights to representation, refrain from unfair influence in labour negotiations or during organising campaigns, and to negotiate constructively on employment conditions. Enterprises are also encouraged to provide reasonable notice of changes in operations that would have major effects upon employees and to co-operate to mitigate these changes' adverse effects.

In the competition area, MNEs are encouraged to conform to countries' rules and policies by, for example, refraining from cartels or restrictive agreements, and from abusing dominant market position through anti-competitive acquisitions, predatory behaviour and other practices.

The Guidelines' recommendations are made in the context of laws, regulations and practices in each of the countries where MNEs operate. The employment and industrial relations guidelines, for example, provide that enterprises should act within the framework of law, regulations, and prevailing labour relations and employment practices in each of the countries where they operate. The Guidelines' recommendations may supplement national law and practice, but can never conflict with it. The recommendations on disclosure of information, for example, go beyond actual practice in most Member countries, setting reasonable and flexible standards for voluntary compliance.

Notes

1. *The OECD Declaration and Decisions on International Investment and Multinational Enterprises - Basic Texts* (OECD Paris, 1992).

2. *The Code of Liberalisation of Capital Movements* (OECD Paris, 1992); see also *Introduction to the OECD Codes of Liberalisation* (OECD Paris, 1987).

Chapter III

HOW THE GUIDELINES WORK

The Guidelines' effectiveness depends on how well they are known, understood and applied. The OECD has established procedures for dealing with the application of the Guidelines in specific cases, for clarifying their purpose and scope, and for making them better known to business, labour, and governments. These procedures are set out in an OECD Council Decision, which is binding on all Members[1]. This chapter explains the institutions and procedures under which the Guidelines' follow-up is undertaken.

1. Institutional arrangements

The OECD Council's Decision on follow-up to the Guidelines, which established procedures for consultation, clarification and review, also identified the institutions responsible for these activities.

a) *National Contact Points*

The National Contact Point (NCP), typically a government office in a Member country, plays a central role in all Guidelines matters.

Member governments have set up National Contact Points to:

-- engage in promotional activities;

-- gather information on experience with the Guidelines;

-- handle enquiries;

-- discuss all matters related to the Guidelines; and

-- assist in solving problems which may arise between business and labour in matters covered by the Guidelines.

These National Contact Points are established under the responsibility of Member governments. The institution chosen to act as Contact Point varies from country to country, as do the activities in which they engage.

One of the Contact Points' most important functions is to act as a forum for discussion on matters relating to the Guidelines. Business and trade unions can discuss problems which may arise from the Guidelines' application and should use the contact as a first step to try and resolve issues at the national level. Co-operation with the NCPs of other countries is an important feature of their work.

b) The OECD Committee on International Investment and Multinational Enterprises (CIME)

The CIME is the OECD's focal point for discussion on foreign investment policy and multinational enterprises. CIME's mandate covers not only the Guidelines but all of the other parts of the 1976 Declaration as well. It was founded in 1975 in response to the need to better analyse and debate policies on international direct investment and multinational enterprises. One year after its founding the CIME had prepared, and OECD Members had adopted, the 1976 Declaration on International Investment and Multinational Enterprises and its related procedural decisions, of which the Guidelines are a part.

The CIME is made up of investment policy officials in OECD Member countries and is staffed by the OECD Directorate for Financial, Fiscal, and Enterprise Affairs. It normally meets twice a year for two or three days. The Commission of the European Communities participates in CIME and Working Group meetings. Hungary, Poland, the Czech Republic, the Slovak Republic and Mexico are observers.

The Committee elects a chairman each year from among its Members. It normally operates on the basis of consensus, although minority reports or dissenting views are possible if consensus cannot be reached. Committee proposals are normally approved by the Council, which is the supreme body of the Organisation and has the power to commit Member countries through legally binding decisions.

Insofar as the Guidelines are concerned, the CIME has a number of specific responsibilities. These include:

-- providing clarifications;

-- proposing changes in the Guidelines and/or the procedural Decisions;

-- regularly reviewing the Guidelines;

-- exchanging views periodically on the role and functioning of the Guidelines;

-- responding to requests from Members on specific or general aspects of the Guidelines;

-- responding to requests from the social partners -- BIAC and TUAC -- on various aspects of the Guidelines; and

-- organising promotional activities like symposiums, seminars and other activities.

The CIME established the Working Group on the Guidelines to prepare its work on Guidelines-related matters. The Working Group normally meets about twice a year to consider questions relating to the Guidelines, and makes recommendations to the CIME. Since 1992 this Working Group has met jointly with the CIME Working Group on Investment Policies.

The CIME's Working Group on Accounting Standards develops clarifications on the accounting terms from the chapter on disclosure of information. Surveys of MNEs' compliance with this chapter's provisions are based on a sample of annual reports from companies in different Member countries. The Working Group also promotes international harmonisation of accounting standards.

Where necessary, the CIME calls on the expertise of other OECD committees to work on specialised topics such as taxation and competition policy. The Committee on Fiscal Affairs has issued guidelines on agreed government approaches towards transfer pricing within associated enterprises and is currently revising and updating the 1979 and 1984 reports on transfer pricing[2]. The Experts' Committee on Restrictive Business Practices, now called the Competition Law and Policy Committee, published a report on MNEs' restrictive business practices[3] and is pursuing its work on different aspects of competition policy and multinational enterprises.

c) ***The Business and Industry Advisory Committee (BIAC) and the Trade Union Advisory Committee (TUAC) to the OECD***

As the Guidelines are addressed to enterprises, business and labour input is especially important. CIME regularly consults with the Business and Industry Advisory Committee (BIAC) and the Trade Union Advisory Committee (TUAC) on matters relating to the Guidelines and on other issues concerning international investment and multinational enterprises.

BIAC and TUAC are accredited to the OECD as official advisory bodies and have as their members business and labour federations in each of the OECD's 24 Member countries. BIAC and TUAC both have secretariats in Paris that are in regular contact with the OECD and Member country delegations.

BIAC and TUAC play an active part in the Guidelines' follow-up procedures by:

-- requesting consultations with National Contact Points on general and specific issues related to the Guidelines' promotion, application or follow-up;

-- raising Guidelines issues at the CIME;

-- informing their Member federations about Guidelines' developments, and seeking members' input on the Guidelines' follow-up procedures; and

-- using their offices to represent business or labour interests to the CIME on matters related to the Guidelines.

In addition, BIAC and TUAC actively participate in various other OECD activities on foreign direct investment, and comment on papers and studies on FDI, as well as participate in other OECD programmes of interest to them.

2. Follow-up procedures

a) *Individual cases*

The Guidelines had to be drafted in fairly general terms since they were to apply to the whole OECD area, with its diversity of legal systems and regulatory traditions, and different practices and approaches towards multinational enterprises. It has therefore been necessary, on occasion, to clarify their purpose and intent, and to provide explanatory comments on various parts of the text which have given rise to questions. A follow-up procedure has been established for this purpose.

The procedure is designed to identify and clarify issues that may arise in the Guidelines' application. When such questions arise, and where a party is unclear about the Guidelines' intention and applicability, that party should, as a first step, approach the National Contact Point (NCP). OECD Member governments, and labour and business organisations, through BIAC and TUAC, may raise such issues.

The National Contact Point should then contact the enterprise, either directly or through the appropriate business federation, to inform it that a Guidelines issue has been raised. The NCP and business and labour representatives should try to resolve the issue at the national level.

If the matter cannot be resolved at the national level because, for example, the issue involves activities in other parts of the enterprise in other Member countries, the Contact Point may pursue bilateral and other contacts to gather and exchange information to try and resolve the matter. In particular, the NCP should contact its counterpart(s) in the country(ies) where the relevant entities of the MNE are located. The NCP of the MNE's headquarters should also be informed.

If a solution to the issue cannot be found through the National Contact Points, and particularly if a clarification seems to be required, the issue can be submitted to the CIME for consideration. Final responsibility for clarifications lies with the Committee, although matters discussed by National Contact Points may sometimes involve questions of the scope and meaning of the Guidelines in specific circumstances. Whenever a Contact Point gives its opinion as to the relevance of the Guidelines to matters at hand, the Contact Point should keep in mind the international character of the Guidelines and the overriding necessity of avoiding conflicting national interpretations. Where there is any doubt or where there are divergent views as to the consistency of an interpretation under consideration by a Contact Point with clarifications adopted by the OECD, the matter should be brought to the attention of the Committee before the Contact Point provides a final answer.

In order to speed up such proceedings, these matters can be referred directly to the Working Group on Investment Policies and the Guidelines for preliminary consideration. After considering the question and consulting with BIAC and TUAC, the CIME may then provide a clarification about how the Guidelines would apply in a situation like the one in question.

The Committee's examination of the need for, and eventual provision of, a clarification uses the details of the specific cases brought before it. The resulting clarification refers to how the Guidelines would apply as concerns the issue raised, however, and is not a judgement on the behaviour of an enterprise, and thus does not refer to the enterprise by name.

This being said, the enterprise concerned may express its views orally or in writing on Guidelines issues involving its interests. Such an enterprise may, alternatively, use the offices of BIAC for this purpose.

Labour and business organisations, through TUAC and BIAC, may themselves submit cases that raise issues for clarification, but an attempt should first be made to resolve the issues at the national level. So far, of the two organisations, only TUAC has made requests for clarifications.

b)   Consultations

The importance of contacts and discussions between those involved with the Guidelines has led to regular consultations between the social partners -- BIAC and TUAC -- and the CIME. These consultations are held at least once a year. In addition, BIAC or TUAC may request a meeting with the CIME to discuss

Guidelines matters at any time, but in practice discussions normally take place during the CIME's regularly scheduled meetings.

c) *Periodic reviews*

OECD Members recognised when the Guidelines were adopted in 1976 that periodic reviews of how the Guidelines were working would improve their effectiveness. Since then, the CIME has carried out reviews in 1979, 1982, 1984, and 1991[4]. These reviews have taken a number of actions to help the Guidelines work better, including improving follow-up procedures, clarifying the Guidelines and amending the text of the Guidelines themselves.

i) *Improving follow-up procedures*

The reviews confirmed the Guidelines as an efficient and realistic framework to further encourage MNEs' contributions to growth and development. Nevertheless, in order to improve awareness and application of the Guidelines the CIME recommended setting up national contact points, establishing a procedure for handling Guidelines matters, allowing BIAC and TUAC to request consultations on Guidelines matters, and providing explanatory comments to give more detail to the Guidelines' provisions and guidance to those using the Guidelines.

One of the most important results of the reviews was to establish National Contact Points, and then to follow-up on how well they were working and make recommendations to improve them. Indeed, the Contact Points' role and functions, the procedures they follow, and countries' experience with them have been extensively studied and discussed. As a result of the review process, the OECD Council modified its Decision on the Guidelines in 1984 to recognise the contacts' role in applying the Guidelines[5].

Another important follow-up theme involved MNEs' experience with the Guidelines and their efforts to promote them. The reviews addressed such questions as whether parent companies and/or subsidiaries should be invited by the Committee to make statements supporting the Guidelines, the frequency with which such statements should be made, how support for the Guidelines should be expressed, and what types of experience companies should report and how. It was agreed that companies' promotional efforts were fundamental in the effort to integrate the Guidelines into management thinking and practice. Many companies have publicly supported the Guidelines' principles and apply them in their own operations.

Structural changes' impact on MNEs' application of the Guidelines has been discussed extensively. A major study was undertaken[6] in which the Guidelines' relevance was recognised in areas covering, for example, employment and industrial relations, science and technology, and disclosure of information. The report recognised that slow economic growth imposed strains for MNEs and their employees, and reiterated the Guidelines' role as a supplement to national law and practice for seeking solutions to restructuring problems, in particular those involving enterprise closures.

Accounting is another area where the reviews have led to substantial follow-up work. The CIME's Working Group on Accounting Standards is responsible for developing clarifications of the accounting terms contained in the chapter on disclosure of information in the Guidelines. The Working Group surveys the extent to which MNEs comply with the provisions of this chapter, based on a sample number of annual reports from companies in different Member countries. The results of these surveys were published in 1987 and 1990. The Working Group also promotes international harmonisation of accounting standards. It sponsors international conferences on subjects of interest to the accounting community in order to maintain a dialogue between governments, non-governmental standard-setting bodies, preparers and users of financial statements, and the accounting profession.

ii) Clarifying the Guidelines

An important function of the reviews is to issue Guidelines clarifications as needed. Clarifications of the Guidelines assist Member governments and multinational enterprises in implementing the Guidelines and ensure their continuing relevance, but do not modify the scope of the Guidelines themselves. They result from a periodic review by the Committee of matters relating to the Guidelines or from discussions initiated at the request of a Member country. While clarifications cover many aspects of the Guidelines, the Committee has had recourse to them primarily in matters of employment and industrial relations, and in the technical accounting items in the disclosure of information chapter.

There is great national diversity in Member countries' labour management policies, including collective bargaining, negotiations, labour management relations, employee representation and the provision of information enabling a true and fair view of the performance of the entity, or the enterprise as a whole, all of which are addressed by the Guidelines. While the Guidelines must be seen in this context of prevailing labour laws, regulations and practices in each of the countries in which multinational enterprises operate, the clarifications have assisted governments and enterprises in interpreting their application to specific cases.

Because of the complexity of multinational enterprises and their diverse structures, operations and policies may not be easy to perceive. This concern can be alleviated by providing greater transparency in their activities through the publication of a body of information on the enterprise as a whole sufficient to improve public understanding. The accounting items in the chapter on disclosure of information contain recommendations on the treatment of operating results, sales, new capital investment, sources and uses of funds, average number of employees, research and development expenditure and segmentation of information. The clarifications have helped enterprises adjust to these standards which, while going further than actual practice in many Member countries, have proven reasonable and flexible standards for voluntary compliance.

iii) Amending the Guidelines

As mentioned above, very few amendments have been made to the Guidelines. A stable set of standards for MNEs has been important to maintaining support for the Guidelines, and also to the Guidelines' contribution to predictability and stability in a rapidly changing investment climate. At the same time, changes in the Guidelines have been necessary from time to time to ensure their continuing relevance.

To the extent that changes have been made, they have resulted from the reviews. It was decided, for example, to amend paragraph 8 of the Employment and Industrial Relations Guidelines (1979 review); paragraph 2 of the General Policies chapter (1984 review); sub-paragraph b) of the Disclosure of Information chapter (1979 review); and to add a new chapter on the environment (1991 review). Each of these changes was made by the OECD Council at CIME's recommendation.

d) Promotional activities

The OECD gives high priority to promoting awareness of the Guidelines. Indeed, it has singled this out as one of the key areas where efforts should be enhanced to ensure that the Guidelines continues to play an effective role. Promotion has become particularly important now that new companies have emerged as important foreign investors and more countries are seeking FDI. These new players need to be aware of the contribution the Guidelines can make in facilitating economically sound and socially advantageous investment.

OECD Members themselves have recognised the importance of promoting the Guidelines and have engaged in a number of activities to make them better known and applied, including:

-- disseminating the Guidelines in national languages;

-- referring to the Guidelines in acts or resolutions of parliamentary bodies;

-- conducting surveys of MNEs' adherence to the Guidelines; and

-- highlighting the Guidelines in informational packages about the countries' foreign investment regime.

Business and labour organisations have also been active in promoting the Guidelines. BIAC has encouraged enterprises to spread knowledge about them through such means as seminars and training courses. BIAC has also advised its Member federations to suggest that their companies disseminate the Guidelines through internal company communications and has published a brochure with comments. Some companies have included a reference to the Guidelines in their annual reports. Labour organisations, through TUAC, have made major efforts to distribute and promote the Guidelines. Employee representatives at the local, national and international level have referred to the Guidelines on a number of occasions when dealing with MNEs.

The OECD's promotional activities have brought together the main players -- business, governments and labour -- to examine new ways of making the Guidelines better known and applied. Recent OECD efforts have targeted new audiences like governments in non-Member countries who want to learn more about attracting socially beneficial and economically sound investment. OECD promotional activities have included:

-- a symposium on the Guidelines to explain their purpose and intent and review experience with the Guidelines;

-- meetings with countries that are not Members of the OECD who want to increase their FDI inflows and generate broad acceptance of FDI, and who see the Guidelines as an element in that effort;

-- publications which contain the Guidelines, and translations of the Guidelines into different languages, including Hungarian, Polish, Czech, Slovak and Russian; and

-- surveys on the role and functioning of the National Contact Points.

Notes

1. *The OECD Declaration and Decisions on International Investment and Multinational Enterprises: Basic Texts* (OECD Paris, 1993).

2. *Transfer Pricing and Multinational Enterprises* (OECD Paris, 1979); *Transfer Pricing and Multinational Enterprises: Three Taxation Issues* (OECD Paris, 1984); *Tax Aspects of Transfer Pricing within Multinational Enterprises: The United States Proposed Regulations* (OECD Paris, 1993).

3. *Restrictive Business Practices of Multinational Enterprises* (OECD Paris, 1977).

4. Full details are available in the review reports. See *OECD Declaration and Decisions on International Investment and Multinational Enterprises: 1979, 1984, 1991 Review Reports* and *1982 Mid-Term Report.*

5. See *The Guidelines for Multinational Enterprises: Second Revised Decision of the Council* (amended June 1991), reproduced in *The OECD Declaration and Decisions on International Investment and Multinational Enterprises: Basic Texts* (OECD Paris, 1992).

6. *Structural Adjustment and Multinational Enterprises* (OECD Paris, 1985).

Chapter IV

COMMENTARY ON THE GUIDELINES

Since their adoption in 1976, Member countries have from time to time reviewed the Guidelines and clarified the meaning of certain terms and references. The Committee on International Investment and Multinational Enterprises is responsible for the clarifications. It may periodically, or at the request of a Member country, hold an exchange of views on matters related to the Guidelines and the experience gained in their application[1]. Clarifications assist governments and multinational enterprises in implementing the Guidelines and ensure the continuing relevance of their provisions. They do not modify the scope of the Guidelines themselves.

The clarifications adopted by the CIME can be found in several published reports reviewing the various parts of the OECD Declaration on International Investment and Multinational Enterprises to which the Guidelines are annexed[2]. The purpose of this chapter is to consolidate these clarifications into one easily accessible text to assist the reader in understanding the Guidelines. This commentary does not modify the clarifications themselves which reflect a complex history and many hours of intensive discussion by the Committee. In any future discussion of a particular issue relating to the Guidelines, the original texts of the clarifications will continue to be regarded as authoritative. There are no comments on the procedures related to the Guidelines nor on experience with the Guidelines. Commentary is preceded by the text of the Guidelines to which they relate.

1. Introduction to the Guidelines

1. *Multinational enterprises now play an important part in the economies of Member countries and in international economic relations, which is of increasing interest to governments. Through international direct investment, such enterprises can bring substantial benefits to home and host countries by contributing to the efficient utilisation of capital,*

27

technology and human resources between countries and can thus fulfil an important role in the promotion of economic and social welfare. But the advances made by multinational enterprises in organising their operations beyond the national framework may lead to abuse of concentrations of economic power and to conflicts with national policy objectives. In addition, the complexity of these multinational enterprises and the difficulty of clearly perceiving their diverse structures, operations and policies sometimes give rise to concern.

2. *The common aim of the Member countries is to encourage the positive contributions which multinational enterprises can make to economic and social progress and to minimise and resolve the difficulties to which their various operations may give rise. In view of the transnational structure of such enterprises, this aim will be furthered by co-operation among the OECD countries where the headquarters of most of the multinational enterprises are established and which are the location of a substantial part of their operations. The Guidelines set out hereafter are designed to assist in the achievement of this common aim and to contribute to improving the foreign investment climate.*

3. *Since the operations of multinational enterprises extend throughout the world, including countries that are not Members of the Organisation, international co-operation in this field should extend to all States. Member countries will give their full support to efforts undertaken in co-operation with non-member countries, and in particular with developing countries, with a view to improving the welfare and living standards of all people both by encouraging the positive contributions which multinational enterprises can make and by minimising and resolving the problems which may arise in connection with their activities.*

4. *Within the Organisation, the programme of co-operation to attain these ends will be a continuing, pragmatic and balanced one. It comes within the general aims of the Convention on the Organisation for Economic Co-operation and Development (OECD) and makes full use of the various specialised bodies of the Organisation, whose terms of reference already cover many aspects of the role of multinational enterprises, notably in matters of international trade and payments, competition, taxation, manpower, industrial development, science and technology. In these bodies, work is being carried out on the identification of issues, the improvement of relevant qualitative and statistical information and the elaboration of proposals for action designed to strengthen inter-governmental co-operation. In some of these areas procedures already exist through which issues related to*

the operations of multinational enterprises can be taken up. This work could result in the conclusion of further and complementary agreements and arrangements between governments.

5. *The initial phase of the co-operation programme is composed of a Declaration and three Decisions promulgated simultaneously as they are complementary and inter-connected, in respect of Guidelines for multinational enterprises, National Treatment for foreign-controlled enterprises and international investment incentives and disincentives.*

6. *The Guidelines set out below are recommendations jointly addressed by Member countries to multinational enterprises operating in their territories. These Guidelines, which take into account the problems which can arise because of the international structure of these enterprises, lay down standards for the activities of these enterprises in the different Member countries. Observance of the Guidelines is voluntary and not legally enforceable. However, they should help to ensure that the operations of these enterprises are in harmony with national policies of the countries where they operate and to strengthen the basis of mutual confidence between enterprises and States.*

7. *Every State has the right to prescribe the conditions under which multinational enterprises operate within its national jurisdiction, subject to international law and to the international agreements to which it has subscribed. The entities of a multinational enterprise located in various countries are subject to the laws of these countries.*

8. *A precise legal definition of multinational enterprises is not required for the purposes of the Guidelines. These usually comprise companies or other entities whose ownership is private, state or mixed, established in different countries and so linked that one or more of them may be able to exercise a significant influence over the activities of others and, in particular, to share knowledge and resources with the others. The degrees of autonomy of each entity in relation to the others varies widely from one multinational enterprise to another, depending on the nature of the links between such entities and the fields of activity concerned. For these reasons, the Guidelines are addressed to the various entities within the multinational enterprise (parent companies and/or local entities) according to the actual distribution of responsibilities among them on the understanding that they will co-operate and provide assistance to one another as necessary to facilitate observance of the Guidelines. The word "enterprise" as used in these Guidelines refers to these various entities in accordance with their responsibilities.*

9. *The Guidelines are not aimed at introducing differences of treatment between multinational and domestic enterprises; wherever relevant*

they reflect good practice for all. Accordingly, multinational and domestic enterprises are subject to the same expectations in respect of their conduct wherever the Guidelines are relevant to both.

10. The use of appropriate international dispute settlement mechanisms, including arbitration, should be encouraged as a means of facilitating the resolution of problems arising between enterprises and Member countries.

11. Member countries have agreed to establish appropriate review and consultation procedures concerning issues arising in respect of the Guidelines. When multinational enterprises are made subject to conflicting requirements by Member countries, the governments concerned will co-operate in good faith with a view to resolving such problems either within the Committee on International Investment and Multinational Enterprises established by the OECD Council on 21 January 1975 or through other mutually acceptable arrangements.

Having regard to the foregoing considerations, the Member countries set forth the following Guidelines for multinational enterprises with the understanding that Member countries will fulfil their responsibilities to treat enterprises equitably and in accordance with international law and international agreements as well as contractual obligations to which they have subscribed.

The Guidelines are recommendations jointly addressed by Member countries to multinational enterprises operating in their territories. They lay down standards for the activities of multinational enterprises and, where relevant, of national enterprises in the different Member countries. Observance of the Guidelines is voluntary and not legally enforceable. They represent, nevertheless, Member countries' firm expectations for multinational enterprise behaviour[3]. Every State has the right to prescribe the conditions under which multinational enterprises operate within its national jurisdiction, subject to international law and the international agreements to which it subscribes. The Guidelines are not a substitute for national laws, to which multinational enterprises are fully subject. They represent supplementary standards of behaviour of a non-legal character, particularly concerning the international operations of these enterprises[4].

The Guidelines do not define the term "multinational enterprises", a concept which embraces a diversity of situations found throughout the business world. Rather, they describe some general criteria covering a broad range of multinational activities and arrangements[5]. These arrangements can include traditional international direct investment based on equity participation, or other means which do not necessarily include an equity capital element. The sharing of knowledge and resources among companies or other entities does not in itself indicate that such companies or entities constitute a multinational enterprise[6]. It is not necessary to determine, in every instance, whether links of a non-equity

30

character between separate entities lead to the conclusion that these entities make up a multinational enterprise.

Since the Guidelines reflect good practice for all enterprises, both multinational and domestic enterprises are subject to the same expectations wherever the Guidelines are relevant to both[7].

Responsibilities of the various entities of a multinational enterprise

All entities, including parent companies, local subsidiaries, as well as intermediary levels of the organisation, are expected to co-operate and assist, as necessary, in observing the Guidelines. To the extent that parent companies actually exercise control over the activities of their subsidiaries, they have a responsibility for observance of the Guidelines by those subsidiaries[8].

The concept of responsibilities of the various entities of a multinational enterprise is relevant for specific paragraphs of the Guidelines, particularly those dealing with the provision of information to employee representatives (see, for example, paragraphs 2 and 3 of the Employment and Industrial Relations chapter of the Guidelines). It is also important to the Guidelines as a whole. The chapter on Disclosure of Information addresses the parent company directly when referring to the publication of "...factual information on the structure, activities and policies of the enterprise as a whole", that is, information which must be gathered and prepared by the parent company. In other areas, such as competition and taxation, observance of the Guidelines may also require that a full picture of the operations of the enterprise as a whole be made available and that enterprises, including parent companies, co-operate with national authorities[9].

The question whether parent companies should assume responsibility for certain financial obligations of subsidiaries as part of good management practice raises complex problems in view of the limited liability principle embodied in Member countries' national laws. The Guidelines cannot supersede or substitute for national laws governing corporate liability. They do not therefore imply an unqualified principle of parent company responsibility. Nonetheless, in certain cases, parent companies have assumed on a voluntary basis financial responsibility for a subsidiary, and such behaviour may actually be considered good management practice under the Guidelines. This question is especially relevant when discussing changes in the operations of a firm and co-operation between the entities to mitigate resulting adverse effects[10].

2.   General policies

Enterprises should:

1.   Take fully into account established general policy objectives of the Member countries in which they operate;

2. *In particular, give due consideration to those countries' aims and priorities with regard to economic and social progress, including industrial and regional development, the protection of the environment and consumer interests, the creation of employment opportunities, the promotion of innovation and the transfer of technology**;

3. *While observing their legal obligations concerning information, supply their entities with supplementary information the latter may need in order to meet requests by the authorities of the countries in which those entities are located for information relevant to the activities of those entities, taking into account legitimate requirements of business confidentiality;*

4. *Favour close co-operation with the local community and business interests;*

5. *Allow their component entities freedom to develop their activities and to exploit their competitive advantage in domestic and foreign markets, consistent with the need for specialisation and sound commercial practice;*

6. *When filling responsible posts in each country of operation, take due account of individual qualifications without discrimination as to nationality, subject to particular national requirements in this respect;*

7. *Not render and they should not be solicited or expected to render any bribe or other improper benefit, direct or indirect, to any public servant or holder of public office;*

8. *Unless legally permissible, not make contributions to candidates for public office or to political parties or other political organisations;*

9. *Abstain from any improper involvement in local political activities.*

The relevance of the initial provisions (paragraphs 1 and 2) is clear when a decision is taken to close down a local subsidiary of a multinational enterprise. While not affecting the right of the enterprise to reach decisions with respect to cutting back or terminating operations in a given plant, a prudent company should seek clarification of government policies through advance consultations with the government concerned[11].

On their part, governments should make sure that their aims and objectives are clear, stable and understandable to management. Although the right of each State to prescribe the operating conditions for multinational enterprises within its

---

* *This paragraph includes the additional provision concerning consumer interests, adopted by the OECD Governments at the meeting of the OECD Council at Ministerial level on 17 and 18 May 1984.*

jurisdiction remains unchanged, such laws and policies are subject to international law and international agreements and should respect contractual obligations. They should also be consistent with Member countries' responsibilities to treat enterprises equitably[12].

This chapter of the Guidelines also recommends that multinational enterprises co-operate closely with the local community and business interests (paragraph 4) and that they allow their various entities freedom to develop and exploit their potential, consistent with the need for specialisation and sound commercial practice (paragraph 5). This argues for a certain amount of integration of the various entities of a multinational enterprise into the economic context of the countries in which they operate. It does not mean that existing structures of multinational enterprises may not be changed, nor does it impinge on the freedom of such enterprises to divest as part of global strategies, if this is considered in the best interests of the firm as a whole. However, this freedom is circumscribed by national law and by a firm's contractual obligations[13].

The question has been raised whether the Guidelines imply that special consideration be given in cases where an enterprise is considering the closing down of a subsidiary or the transfer of its activities abroad, especially if the particular subsidiary is a profitable one. In practice, the profitability of a particular entity may be difficult to evaluate due to the different accounting standards and practices used to determine value and future profitability. However, whenever there is clear evidence of the profitability of a particular subsidiary, the company should give special consideration to this fact when contemplating the closing down of that subsidiary. This does not restrict the company's right to make such a decision which may take account of other factors besides profitability[14].

The international expansion of trade and other technological developments, such as product packaging, marketing and sales products and product safety, can affect consumer policies. All OECD Member countries have adopted policies aimed at protecting consumer interests. This includes issues of consumer safety which are also covered by an OECD Council Recommendation[15]. Paragraph 2 of this chapter recognises the international aspects of consumer policies. Many of the international issues related to consumer protection may not be particular to multinational enterprises and should be handled through consumer protection legislation in Member countries.

Where issues arise which are not covered by national legislation, multinational enterprises should give due consideration to Member countries' interests in the area of consumer protection. This may include ensuring, where possible, uniform quality of a particular product sold under a specific trademark, regardless of where it is produced, subject to local requirements[16].

3. **Disclosure of information**

Enterprises should, having due regard to their nature and relative size in the economic context of their operations and to requirements of business confidentiality and to cost, publish in a form suited to improve public understanding a sufficient body of factual information on the structure, activities and policies of the enterprise as a whole, as a supplement, in so far as necessary for this purpose, to information to be disclosed under the supplement, in so far as necessary for this purpose, to information to be disclosed under the national law of the individual countries in which they operate. To this end, they should publish within reasonable time limits, on a regular basis, but at least annually, financial statements and other pertinent information relating to the enterprise as a whole, comprising in particular:

a) *The structure of the enterprise, showing the name and location of the parent company, its main affiliates, its percentage ownership, direct and indirect, in these affiliates, including shareholdings between them;*

b) *The geographical areas* where operations are carried out and the principal activities carried on therein by the parent company and the main affiliates;*

c) *The operating results and sales by geographical area and the sales in the major line of business for the enterprise as a whole;*

d) *Significant new capital investment by geographical area and, as far as practicable, by major lines of business for the enterprise as a whole;*

e) *A statement of the sources and uses of funds by the enterprise as a whole;*

f) *The average number of employees in each geographical area;*

g) *Research and development expenditure for the enterprise as a whole;*

h) *The policies followed in respect of intra-group pricing;*

---

* *For the purposes of the Guideline on Disclosure of Information the term "geographical area" means groups of countries or individual countries as each enterprise determines is appropriate in its particular circumstances. While no single method of grouping is appropriate for all enterprises or for all purposes, the factors to be considered by an enterprise would include the significance of geographic proximity, economic affinity, similarities in business environments and the nature, scale and degree of interrelationship of the enterprises' operations in the various countries. [This text is an integral part of the negotiated instruments.]*

i)   *The accounting policies, including those on consolidation, observed in compiling the published information.*

The purpose of this chapter is to encourage greater transparency of the enterprise as a whole through the publication of a body of information sufficient to improve public understanding[17]. This can alleviate concerns arising from the complexity of multinational enterprises and the difficulties in clearly perceiving their diverse structures, operations and policies[18].

Some enterprises expressed concern with this chapter, reflecting either difficulties of adjustment or revealing problems of a more conceptual nature. The following problem areas were identified:

i)   The disclosure of certain types of information (cf. operating results by geographical area) may result in competitive disadvantages, especially for firms which have only one or a few customers in a particular country or region. In this regard, the Guidelines on disclosure contain qualifications which make allowances for the specific situations of companies in the context of their operations. Other than in very exceptional circumstances, these qualifications are not intended as complete or permanent exemptions from certain disclosure standards and should be invoked only for valid reasons;

ii)   Reference was also made to cost and time factors involved in changing or supplementing existing reporting practices, in particular for smaller companies with limited international experience. The chapter on Disclosure of Information makes specific allowances for factors such as cost and relative size of the company. The Guidelines therefore provide flexibility for adjusting reporting practices over a reasonable period of time;

iii)   The Guidelines recognise the diversity of national reporting and accounting requirements with respect to the items contained in this chapter. These recommendations are intended to supplement, where necessary, the disclosure and reporting requirements laid down by national law to increase public understanding "on the structure, activities and the policies of the enterprises as a whole". National requirements which are less comprehensive should not prevent multinational enterprises from implementing the Guidelines. In the absence of internationally agreed accounting standards, such reports will follow the accounting principles generally accepted in the country in which the parent company, or a controlling entity at the intermediary level, is domiciled. It is important that companies state the accounting principles which have been used;

iv)   Problems were also raised with respect to segmentation of information. In particular, there are doubts as to whether disclosure by "geographical area" is the most appropriate method of segmentation. The Guidelines, however, leave some degree of flexibility for companies to determine the most appropriate geographical breakdown. This may be an issue where the interests of some users of the published data differ in some cases from those of the enterprises, which may find a line of business approach more useful for internal purposes. Nevertheless, the Guidelines reflect the value Member governments place on geographical segmentation of information[19].

These disclosure recommendations go beyond actual practice in most Member countries, and adjustment may present difficulties and cost. These recommendations are nevertheless reasonable and sufficiently flexible. They confirm the importance Member countries attach to the objectives of this chapter[20].

A number of accounting terms and disclosure items in this chapter required further explanation to assist enterprises in complying with them. Clarifications of many of the items included in this chapter -- e.g. operating results, sales, new capital investment, sources and uses of funds, average number of employees, research and development expenditure, accounting policies and segmentation of information -- were published in the brochure *Multinational Enterprises and Disclosure of Information: Clarification of the OECD Guidelines* (OECD, 1988). The special characteristics of some specific sectors, such as banking and insurance, and the applicability of certain concepts of information disclosure to their operations, are also treated in this publication.

The following paragraphs describe only those clarifications adopted since the 1988 publication which remains relevant for all issues relating to the disclosure of information.

The Guidelines indicate a general objective of disclosure of information which is to increase transparency of the structure, policies and activities of multinational enterprises. Promoting harmonisation of international accounting and reporting practices is an important element in meeting those objectives and is the main responsibility of the CIME's Working Group on Accounting Standards.

In 1988, the Working Group evaluated the accounting and reporting issues arising from new financial instruments in light of their economic importance and implications both for banks and non-banking enterprises. The results of this work led to the conclusion that the Disclosure of Information chapter is comprehensive and flexible enough to deal with the disclosure and accounting issues relating to new financial instruments. The list of specific information items set out in the chapter is illustrative and non-exclusive and can therefore cover disclosure of significant off-balance sheet risks associated with new financial instruments[21].

4. Competition

Enterprises should, while conforming to official competition rules and established policies of the countries in which they operate:

1. *Refrain from actions which would adversely affect competition in the relevant market by abusing a dominant position of market power, by means of, for example:*

   a) *Anti-competitive acquisitions;*

   b) *Predatory behaviour toward competitors;*

   c) *Unreasonable refusal to deal;*

   d) *Anti-competitive abuse of industrial property rights;*

   e) *Discriminatory (i.e. unreasonably differentiated) pricing and using such pricing transactions between affiliated enterprises as a means of affecting adversely competition outside these enterprises;*

2. *Allow purchasers, distributors and licensees freedom to resell, export, purchase and develop their operations consistent with law, trade conditions, the need for specialisation and sound commercial practice;*

3. *Refrain from participating in or otherwise purposely strengthening the restrictive effects of international or domestic cartels or restrictive agreements which adversely affect or eliminate competition and which are not generally or specifically accepted under applicable national or international legislation;*

4. *Be ready to consult and co-operate, including the provision of information, with competent authorities of countries whose interests are directly affected in regard to competition issues or investigations. Provisions of information should be in accordance with safeguards normally applicable in this field.*

The chapter on Competition represents a common approach to competition problems in the OECD area. Enterprises should conform to the competition rules and policies of the countries in which they operate and refrain from actions which would adversely affect competition.

While restrictive business practices engaged in by multinational enterprises are no different from those practised by national enterprises, they may impact more significantly on trade and competition and on the process of national and international concentration because of the more international character of their operations. The complex legal and economic issues involved in this area, such as abuse of a dominant position, adverse effects on competition, and unreasonably differentiated pricing policies, means that the Guidelines alone cannot provide precise rules for business executives to follow. The national law of various countries has given meaning to these concepts through interpretation by the competent tribunals[22].

Also relevant are the 1986 OECD Council Recommendation concerning co-operation between Member countries on restrictive business practices affecting international trade[23] and the United Nations Set of Multilaterally Agreed Equitable Principles and Rules for the Control of Restrictive Business Practices. The United Nations Rules have a greater degree of specificity in the areas covered and as such can be seen as an illustration of the same principles as those embodied in the Guidelines. The responsibilities for follow-up procedures under the Guidelines and the UN Rules are, however, institutionally separate[24].

5.   Financing

Enterprises should, in managing the financial and commercial operations of their activities, and especially their liquid foreign assets and liabilities, take into consideration the established objectives of the countries in which they operate regarding balance of payments and credit policies.

[There are no clarifications of this paragraph.]

6.   Taxation

Enterprises should:

1. *Upon request of the taxation authorities of the countries in which they operate provide, in accordance with the safeguards and relevant procedures of the national laws of these countries, the information necessary to determine correctly the taxes to be assessed in connection with their operations, including relevant information concerning their operations in other countries;*

2. *Refrain from making use of the particular facilities available to them, such as transfer pricing which does not conform to an arm's length standard, for modifying in ways contrary to national laws the tax base on which members of the group are assessed.*

The first paragraph deals with the supplying, upon request, of relevant information concerning the operations of related entities in other countries to national tax authorities in one country. This recommendation can be a useful supplement to the means that national tax authorities have at their disposal for securing information on activities of multinational enterprises abroad. These requests should be in line with generally recognised practices[25].

The use of transfer pricing to modify, in ways contrary to national law, the tax base on which members of the group are assessed is covered by the second paragraph of this chapter. No specific clarifications of this paragraph have been developed; however, the OECD Council did approve a Recommendation to Member governments[26] advising their tax authorities to take into account, when reviewing and, if necessary, adjusting transfer prices between associated enterprises for the purposes of determining taxable profits, the considerations and methods set out in a Report by the Committee on Fiscal Affairs[27] on the determination of transfer prices between associated enterprises for arriving at arm's-length prices when goods, technology, trademarks and services are provided or supplied, or loans granted, between associated enterprises.

7. Employment and industrial relations

While the Guidelines cover all major aspects of corporate behaviour, the ILO Tripartite Declaration of Principles concerning Multinationals and Social Policy (1977) sets out principles only in the fields of employment, training, conditions of work and industrial relations which governments, employers and workers, as well as multinational enterprises, are recommended to observe. Wherever these principles refer to the behaviour expected by multinational enterprises they parallel the OECD Guidelines and do not conflict with them. They can therefore be of use in understanding the Guidelines to the extent that they are of a greater degree of elaboration. However, the responsibilities for the follow-up procedures under the Tripartite Declaration and the Guidelines are institutionally separate[28].

a) *Introductory clause*

Enterprises should, within the framework of law, regulations and prevailing labour relations and employment practices, in each of the countries in which they operate:

This important introductory paragraph is to be read in conjunction with each of the separate paragraphs in the chapter on Employment and Industrial Relations.

b) *Employee representation*

1. Respect the right of their employees to be represented by trade unions and other bona fide organisations of employees, and engage in constructive negotiations, either individually or through employers' associations, with such employee organisations with a view to reaching agreements on employment conditions, which should include provisions for dealing with disputes arising over the interpretation of such agreements, and for ensuring mutually respected rights and responsibilities;

This paragraph expressly provides for management engaging in constructive negotiations on employment conditions with employee representatives. The thrust of the Guidelines in this area is towards management adopting a positive approach towards the activities of trade unions and other bona fide organisations of employees of all categories and, in particular, an open attitude towards organisational activities of workers within the framework of national rules and practices[29].

The Guidelines do not indicate what organisations in a specific sense should represent employees for collective bargaining purposes or what criteria should be used for the selection of such organisations[30]. The Guidelines will not put obstacles in the way of recognition by management, in agreement with national laws and practices, of an International Trade Secretariat as a "bona fide organisation of employees"[31].[*]

Although the question is not directly addressed, this paragraph implies that management should adopt a co-operative attitude towards the participation of employees in international meetings for consultation and exchanges of views among themselves provided that the functioning of the enterprise's operations and the normal procedures governing relationships with employee representatives and their organisations are not prejudiced thereby[32].

c)   *Providing assistance and information to employee representatives*

     2.   **a)**   ***Provide such facilities to representatives of the employees as may be necessary to assist in the development of effective collective agreements;***

           b)   ***Provide to representatives of employees information which is needed for meaningful negotiations on conditions of employment;***

The positive attitude towards employee representation encouraged by the Guidelines is also expressed in this paragraph which recommends that management provide facilities to employee representatives as necessary to assist in developing effective collective agreements and the information needed for meaningful negotiations on employment conditions. The term "meaningful" must be applied in the circumstances of each case, but it has operational value to persons experienced in labour relations[33].

Negotiations, consultations, co-operation or the provision of information to employees implies effective communication between the parties concerned. As a general rule, management and labour representatives should communicate in a

---

[*]   *The Committee did not consider the question of the conduct of collective bargaining at an international level, for which there are no real examples, although there has been some development of trade union effort to co-ordinate approaches to MNEs on a cross-country basis.*

language effectively understood by employees or their representatives. Where this may be unreasonably difficult, such as when representatives from the parent company are involved, adequate interpretation and translation facilities should be provided[34].

d) *Providing information for a true and fair view*

3. ***Provide to representatives of employees where this accords with local law and practice, information which enables them to obtain a true and fair view of the performance of the entity or, where appropriate, the enterprise as a whole;***

In accordance with local law and practice, employee representatives should be given information which enables them to obtain a true and fair view of the performance of the entity or, where appropriate, the enterprise as a whole. Where employee representatives experience difficulties in obtaining such information at the national level because the entity in that country is unable to comply with the provisions of paragraphs 2 and 3, the other entities of the enterprise are expected to co-operate and assist one another as necessary to facilitate observance of the Guidelines[35].[*]

i) *Subjects covered by the information to be supplied*

The laws, regulations and practices in Member countries with respect to the provision of information by enterprises to employees differ considerably. In some countries, statutory provisions are very extensive and detailed, whereas in others, management and labour representatives define, on the basis of need, the information which management is expected to provide on a "good faith basis". There is no general approach to this question as illustrated by the many facets of information provision, including the type of information to be provided, its degree of detail, whether provided to the individual entity or the group (national or international), the timing of provision, whether it covers present situation and past developments and/or future outlook, etc.[36]

Because of this diversity in Member country situations, it is neither feasible nor practical to give an authoritative and detailed list of items covered by the expression "information enabling a true and fair view of the performance of the entity and, where appropriate, the enterprise as a whole"[37]. While the Disclosure of Information Guidelines address the provision of information to the general public, employees of multinational enterprises may need and should have access to more specific information, beyond that available to the general public, and in

---

[*]   *This clarification is relevant for both paragraph 2b and paragraph 3.*

a form suitable for their interests and purposes[38]. Enterprises should provide information on aspects of the performance of the enterprise which will also enable users to assess, *inter alia*, likely future developments. In so doing, they should be guided by the information items enumerated in the Disclosure of Information chapter of the Guidelines[39].

Where more specific information is necessary, management and labour should be prepared to discuss information requirements in a constructive manner, taking account of the specific situation of the enterprise and of local laws, regulations and practices. Considerations of business confidentiality may mean that information on certain points may not be provided, or may not be provided without safeguards[40].

ii) *Restructuring activities and the position of the enterprise as a whole*

Certain activities of multinational enterprises, for instance restructuring activities, can be put into perspective only if the information on the position of the enterprise as a whole is available. If restructuring, or similar decisions, results in negotiations where the position of the enterprise as a whole is a key element, then employee representatives should have the information which gives a true and fair view of the enterprise as a whole and which they need for meaningful negotiation on employment conditions. As noted above, the provision of information is subject to considerations of business confidentiality[41].

e) *Standards of employment*

4. *Observe standards of employment and industrial relations not less favourable than those observed by comparable employers in the host country;*

[There are no clarifications of this paragraph.]

f) *Use, training, and preparing for upgrading members of local labour force*

5. *In their operations, to the greatest extent practicable, utilise, train and prepare for upgrading members of the local labour force in co-operation with representatives of their employees and, where appropriate, the relevant governmental authorities;*

[There are no clarifications of this paragraph.]

g) Providing reasonable notice of changes in operations

6. *In considering changes in their operations which would have major effects upon the livelihood of their employees, in particular in the case of the closure of an entity involving collective lay-offs or dismissals, provide reasonable notice of such changes to representatives of their employees, and where appropriate to the relevant governmental authorities and co-operate with the employee representatives and appropriate governmental authorities so as to mitigate to the maximum extent practicable adverse effects;*

i) Taking account of established policy objectives

This paragraph must be read together with the General Policies chapter which provides that enterprises take account of the established general policy objectives of Member countries in which they operate and their economic and social priorities. In particular, paragraph 2 of the General Policies chapter provides guidance to multinational enterprises as to how they should take account of the interests of the countries in which they operate whenever major cross-border restructuring activities are carried out[42].

When a local subsidiary of a multinational enterprise is to be closed down, a company should seek all necessary information on the country's relevant aims and practices from the government concerned. While this does not affect the right of the enterprise to reach decisions with respect to cutting back or terminating operations in a given plant, certain considerations should be carefully weighed in making such a decision[43].

ii) Reasonable notice

Reasonable notice is linked to the recommendation that management co-operate with employee representatives and governmental authorities in order to mitigate the adverse effects of such changes. For such notice to be "reasonable", it should be sufficiently timely for the purpose of mitigating action to be prepared and put into effect[44]. Notice of changes should be given and the actual changes implemented in such a way that meaningful co-operation can take place. It would conform to the general intention of this paragraph, in light of the specific circumstances of each case, if management were able to give such notice prior to the final decision being taken[45].

These are not intended as rigid rules which would make management's task more difficult. The Guidelines recognise that the sensitivity of certain business decisions and/or of particular jobs, in terms of possible serious damage to a particular enterprise, is such that it is difficult for management, when considering changes in activities which would have major effects on the livelihood of their

43

employees, to give employee representatives early notice of such changes. However, these considerations would only apply in exceptional circumstances. There is no business sector or business activity where such circumstances can be considered usual[46].

iii) Employee representatives

On occasion, enterprises may be faced with a situation where their employees are not represented by trade unions and other bona fide employee organisations. In such cases, enterprises should take all practical steps towards meeting the objectives underlying paragraph 6, within the framework of national laws, regulations and prevailing labour relations practices[47].

h) Non-discrimination

7. *Implement their employment policies including hiring, discharge, pay, promotion and training without discrimination unless selectivity in respect of employee characteristics is in furtherance of established governmental policies which specifically promote greater equality of employment opportunity;*

[There are no clarifications of this paragraph.]

i) Unfair influence

8. *In the context of bona fide negotiations* with representatives of employees on conditions of employment, or while employees are exercising a right to organise, not threaten to utilise a capacity to transfer the whole or part of an operating unit from the country concerned nor transfer employees from the enterprises' component entities in other countries in order to influence unfairly those negotiations or to hinder the exercise of a right to organise;***

---

* *Bona fide negotiations may include labour disputes as part of the process of negotiation. Whether or not labour disputes are so included will be determined by the law and prevailing employment practices of particular countries. [This text is an integral part of the negotiated instruments.]*

** *This paragraph includes the additional provision, concerning transfer of employees, adopted by OECD Governments at the meeting of the OECD Council at Ministerial level on 13 and 14 June 1979.*

This paragraph was meant to cover only operations involving existing plant and equipment. Nevertheless, future investments, such as replacement of equipment or the introduction of new technology, may be crucial to the survival of the enterprises in the medium and long term and thus may be of interest in this context[48].

A distinction should be made between information given to employees on the likely consequences for the future of the firm as a going concern for the eventual outcome of such negotiations, which is legitimately provided by management, and threats which would be an unfair use of management's negotiating power. "Unfair" is the key notion in this context. It is appropriate for management to inform employee representatives if certain demands have, in their view, serious implications for the economic viability of the enterprise. Management should, nevertheless, be prepared to support this claim with appropriate information[49].

j) Conduct of negotiations

9. Enable authorised representatives of their employees to conduct negotiations on collective bargaining or labour management relations issues with representatives of management who are authorised to take decisions on the matters under negotiation.

When negotiations or collective bargaining take place in the context of a parent-subsidiary relationship, the subsidiary may not be fully empowered to negotiate and to conclude an agreement. There may be special problems in the case of a subsidiary situated in a country different from that of the parent company. In these situations, the parent company is expected to take the necessary organisational steps to enable its subsidiaries to observe the Guidelines, *inter alia*, by providing adequate and timely information and ensuring that the enterprise's representatives carrying out such negotiations at the national or local level are duly authorised to take decisions on matters under negotiation. The management of a multinational enterprise should see that this is observed in the circumstances of each case[50].

Where relevant national law provides for negotiations prior to final decisions being reached, employee representatives should be given an opportunity to conduct negotiations with authorised management before major decisions are predetermined through co-ordination and/or contractual arrangements between the enterprises concerned[51].

i) "Collective bargaining" and "Labour management relations"

There exists no internationally agreed standard of the scope of the terms "collective bargaining" and "labour management relations". In fact, there is wide diversity among Member countries concerning national practices with respect to both of these.

In some countries, collective bargaining or labour-management relations are limited to conditions of employment in a more traditional sense (for example, wages, working hours, health and safety standards). In other countries, there is a trend towards including information and consultations on the economic and financial management of the enterprise, extending to future production and investment plans to some extent. As they are used in the Guidelines, the terms are sufficiently broad to permit a variety of interpretations in light of different national situations. Their specific meaning is determined by reference to national law, regulations and prevailing labour relations and employment practices in each country[52].

ii) "Negotiations"

The Guidelines do not define what is meant by "negotiations". As a general rule, it implies an effort to reach agreement by the parties concerned. It may, however, be difficult in practice to distinguish between "negotiations" and "consultations", the latter term in some countries being used in situations where management retains the prerogative of a final decision in case of disagreement, after listening to the views of employee representatives. In some cases, "consultations" may be understood to imply an effort to reach agreement, although management retains final decision-making power[53].

Paragraph 9 does not institute a claim for opening consultations or negotiations in the absence of other relevant provisions. It supposes that such consultations or negotiations are conducted in the framework of national laws and practices of the country where the entity of the multinational enterprise is located. When interpreting the Employment and Industrial Relations chapter, and in particular paragraph 9, the precise sense of "consultation" or "negotiation" should be defined by these laws and practices[54].

iii) Future production and investment matters

When dealing with the specific issue of consultation or negotiations in which future production and investment plans are involved, paragraph 9 avoids the need for defining the locus of the negotiations or the proper level of management to be involved in such negotiations. This depends on the decision-making structure of each multinational enterprise. Negotiations conducted in accordance with national practice should take place in a meaningful manner with management representatives in a position to directly influence decisions on investment matters and to engage in effective negotiations. Where negotiations are defined by national practice in a way that management, in case of disagreement, remains free to make the final decision, these negotiations should still provide employee representatives the opportunity to discuss with management representatives who have a real impact upon the final decision[55].

Management has a range of possibilities from which to choose to enable meaningful negotiations between management and employee representatives. Its choice depends on various circumstances, such as the matters under discussion, the decision-making structure within the enterprise, and the importance of the decision to be taken. Examples of these possibilities include:

-- to provide the management of the subsidiary with adequate and timely information and to ensure that it has sufficient powers to conduct meaningful negotiations with employee representatives;

-- to nominate one or more representatives of the decision-making centre to the negotiating team of the subsidiary in order to ensure that management has sufficient power to conduct meaningful negotiations with employee representatives;

-- to engage directly in negotiations[56].

iv) Information on the decision-making structure of the enterprise

The Guidelines do not imply an unqualified right of employees to be informed about the decision-making structure within the enterprise. However, for meaningful negotiations to take place, employee representatives have a legitimate interest to be informed about the decision-making structure within the enterprise in the negotiating situations referred to in the Guidelines, and in particular, paragraph 9[57].

8. Environmental protection[58]

Enterprises should, within the framework of laws, regulations and administrative practices in the countries in which they operate, and recalling the provisions of paragraph 9 of the Introduction to the Guidelines that, inter alia, multinational and domestic enterprises are subject to the same expectations in respect of their conduct whenever the Guidelines are relevant to both, take due account of the need to protect the environment and avoid creating environmentally related health problems. In particular, enterprises, whether multinational or domestic, should:

1. Assess, and take into account in decision making, foreseeable environmental and environmentally related health consequences of their activities, including siting decisions, impact on indigenous natural resources and foreseeable environmental and environmentally related health risks of products as well as from the generation, transport and disposal of waste;

2. *Co-operate with competent authorities, inter alia, by providing adequate and timely information regarding the potential impacts on the environment and environmentally related health aspects of all their activities and by providing the relevant expertise available in the enterprise as a whole;*

3. *Take appropriate measures in their operations to minimise the risk of accidents and damage to health and the environment, and to co-operate in mitigating adverse effects, in particular:*

    a) *by selecting and adopting those technologies and practices which are compatible with these objectives;*

    b) *by introducing a system of environmental protection at the level of the enterprise as a whole including, where appropriate, the use of environmental auditing;*

    c) *by enabling their component entities to be adequately equipped, especially by providing them with adequate knowledge and assistance;*

    d) *by implementing education and training programmes for their employees;*

    e) *by preparing contingency plans; and*

    f) *by supporting, in an appropriate manner, public information and community awareness programmes.*

Public awareness and concerns about the environment have increased steadily since the Guidelines were first adopted in 1976. The development of national environmental protection policies in OECD countries reflects this concern. In view of increasing economic and technological interdependence, environmental protection has developed a strong international dimension. Certain problems of a bilateral, regional or global significance cannot be dealt with adequately within a national context; their solution depends on international co-operation and agreement.

The Guidelines' General Policies chapter recommends that enterprises give due consideration to host countries' aims and policies with regard to environmental protection. The Committee developed a clarification on the environment in 1985 and, in reviewing the Guidelines in 1991, decided that a new chapter on environmental protection should be included in the Guidelines closely following this clarification.

This decision was based on a number of considerations. A separate chapter has higher visibility than a clarification and is more indicative of the significance given to environmental concerns by Member countries. The chapter recognises the links between economic and environmental objectives and is a concrete reflection of the evolution of environmental awareness in industry. Indeed, the climate and tone of industry-government relationships in the area of environment has evolved and increasingly provides an example of co-operation.

Protecting the environment is a general concern not limited to the actions of enterprises. Indeed, governments must define their economic and development goals in this context. In introducing this chapter, the CIME stressed the importance of the role played by government and the need to make its objectives as clear, stable and understandable as possible to management, and of harmonising environmental policies where valid reasons for differences do not exist.

The relationship between good safety and health procedures related to the work place and the protection of the environment is also covered in this new chapter, which includes a reference to the need to avoid creating environmentally related health problems. The CIME has recalled that issues concerning safety and health are also dealt with in the *ILO Tripartite Declaration of Principles* concerning Multinational Enterprises and Social Policy, which is considered relevant in this respect.

This chapter does not single out multinational enterprises for special attention. On the contrary, a key feature of the Guidelines is their non-discriminatory nature. The Guidelines do not imply differences in the treatment or behaviour of multinational and domestic enterprises or that particular enterprises should adhere to higher standards -- both groups of enterprises are subject to the same expectations with respect to their conduct whenever the Guidelines are relevant to both. In fact, the technological knowledge of multinational enterprises puts them in the forefront of environmental protection efforts, and governments welcome their continued support of public authorities in this area.

9. Science and technology

Enterprises should:

1. *Endeavour to ensure that their activities fit satisfactorily into the scientific and technological policies and plans of the countries in which they operate, and contribute to the development of national scientific and technological capacities, including as far as appropriate the establishment and improvement in host countries of their capacity to innovate;*

2. *To the fullest extent practicable, adopt in the course of their business activities practices which permit the rapid diffusion of technologies*

with due regard to the protection of industrial and intellectual property rights;

3. *When granting licenses for the use of industrial property rights or when otherwise transferring technology, do so on reasonable terms and conditions.*

The chapter aims to promote, within the limits of economic feasibility and other considerations, the distribution by multinational enterprises of research and development activities among the countries where they operate, contributing thereby to the innovative capacities of host countries.   It also urges multinational enterprises to rapidly diffuse the results of their research and development activities on reasonable terms and conditions.

When considering changes in their operations, enterprises should endeavour to ensure that their entities are not unduly deprived of resources for technological development directly related to their manufacturing and marketing role in the group as a whole.   Enterprises should encourage the establishment and improvement of their innovative capacity and, bearing in mind the need for sound commercial practices, develop in their component entities a capability for technological innovation[59].

Notes

1. See *Second Revised Decision of the Council on the Guidelines for Multinational Enterprises*, paragraph 3, reproduced in Annex 2 to this report.

2. *International Investment in Multinational Enterprises, Review of the 1976 Declaration and Decisions* (OECD Paris, 1979); *The Mid-Term Report on the 1976 Declaration and Decisions* (OECD Paris, 1982); and *The 1984 Review of the 1976 Declaration and Decisions* (OECD Paris, 1984). *The OECD Declaration and Decisions on International Investment and Multinational Enterprises, 1991 Review* (OECD Paris, 1992).

3. Chapter II, paragraph 3, *The OECD Guidelines for Multinational Enterprises* (OECD Paris, 1986).

4. *ibid*, Chapter II, paragraph 4.

5. The Guidelines are addressed to enterprises (private, state, mixed) "established in different countries and so linked that one or more of them may be able to exercise a significant influence over the activities of others and, in particular, to share knowledge and resources with the others"; *ibid*, Chapter II, paragraph 5.

6. *ibid*, Chapter II, paragraphs 5 and 9. See also page 48, *The OECD Declaration and Decisions on International Investment and Multinational Enterprises, 1991 Review* (OECD Paris, 1992).

7. Chapter II, paragraph 6, *The OECD Guidelines*, *op. cit.* at note 3.

8. *ibid*, Chapter II, paragraph 5.

9. *ibid*, Chapter II, paragraph 7.

10. *ibid*, Chapter II, paragraph 8.

11. *ibid*, Chapter II, paragraph 10.

12. *ibid*, Chapter II, paragraph 11.

13. *ibid*, Chapter II, paragraph 12.

14. *ibid*, Chapter II, paragraph 12.

15. *The OECD Council Recommendation Covering the Safety of Consumer Products*, 18 December 1979.

16. Chapter II, paragraphs 14-15, *The OECD Guidelines*, *op. cit.* at note 3.

17. Page 44, *The OECD Declaration and Decisions, 1991 Review*, *op. cit.* at note 6.

18. Chapter II, paragraph 29, *The OECD Guidelines*, *op. cit.* at note 3.

19. *ibid*, Chapter II, paragraph 31.

20. *ibid*, Chapter II, paragraph 33.

21. Page 46, *The OECD Declaration and Decisions, 1991 Review*, *op. cit.* at note 6.

22. Chapter II, paragraph 43, *The OECD Guidelines*, *op. cit.* at note 3.

23. Recommendation of the OECD Council, 21 May 1986. A further Recommendation on Co-operation between Member Countries in Areas of Potential Conflict Between Competition and Trade Policies was adopted by the Council on 23 October 1986.

24. Chapter II, paragraph 47, *The OECD Guidelines*, *op. cit.* at note 3.

25. *ibid*, Chapter II, paragraph 50.

26. Recommendation of the OECD Council on the Determination of Transfer Prices Between Associated Enterprises, 16 May 1979.

27. *Transfer Pricing and Multinational Enterprises* (OECD Paris, 1979). A task force has been set up to review the recommendations in this Report taking account of recent developments.

28. Chapter II, paragraph 177, *The OECD Guidelines, op. cit.* at note 3. See also Tripartite Declaration of Principles concerning Multinationals and Social Policy (ILO, 1977).

29. Chapter II, paragraphs 54 and 83. See also page 43, *The OECD Declaration and Decisions, 1991 Review, op. cit.* at note 6.

30. Chapter II, paragraph 54, *The OECD Guidelines, op. cit.* at note 3.

31. *ibid*, Chapter II, paragraph 56.

32. *ibid*, Chapter II, paragraph 55.

33. *ibid*, Chapter II, paragraph 58.

34. *ibid*, Chapter II, paragraph 84.

35. *ibid*, Chapter II, paragraph 59.

36. Page 47, *The OECD Declaration and Decisions, 1991 Review, op. cit.* at note 6.

37. Chapter II, paragraph 58, *The OECD Guidelines, op. cit.* at note 3 and page 47, *The OECD Declaration and Decisions, 1991 Review, op. cit.* at note 6.

38. Chapter II, paragraph 86, *The OECD Guidelines, op. cit.* at note 3 and page 47, *The OECD Declaration and Decisions, 1991 Review, op. cit.* at note 6.

39. Pages 46-47, *The OECD Declaration and Decisions, 1991 Review, op. cit.* at note 6.

40. *ibid*, page 48.

41. Chapter II, paragraph 87, *The OECD Guidelines, op. cit.* at note 3 and page 47, *The OECD Declaration and Decisions, op. cit.* at note 6.

42. Pages 48-49, *The OECD Declaration and Decisions, 1991 Review, op. cit.* at note 6.

43. *ibid*, page 49.

44. Chapter II, paragraphs 60-61, *The OECD Guidelines, op. cit.* at note 6.

45. Page 49, *The OECD Declaration and Decisions*, 1991 Review, *op. cit.* at note 6.

46. *ibid*, page 44.

47. *ibid*, page 43.

48. Chapter II, paragraph 62, *The OECD Guidelines, op. cit.* at note 3.

49. *ibid*, Chapter II, paragraph 63.

50. *ibid*, Chapter II, paragraphs 65-66.

51. *ibid*, Chapter II, paragraph 79.

52. *ibid*, Chapter II, paragraph 72.

53. *ibid*, Chapter II, paragraph 74.

54. *ibid*, Chapter II, paragraph 75.

55. *ibid*, Chapter II, paragraph 77.

56. *ibid*, Chapter II, paragraph 78.

57. *ibid*, Chapter II, paragraphs 80-81.

58. This clarification is contained in pages 52-54 of *The OECD Declaration and Decisions, 1991 Review, op. cit.* at note 6.

59. Chapter II, paragraph 90, *The OECD Guidelines, op. cit.* at note 3.

Chapter V

CONCLUSION

The Guidelines experience has been positive. As an OECD instrument it has covered the bulk of investment world-wide, receiving support from companies, countries and labour unions active in the international investment process. As part of a comprehensive package for the treatment of international investment, it has helped develop understanding between business, government and labour about what can reasonably be expected of MNEs in foreign markets.

As with any internationally negotiated instrument, the Guidelines have sometimes been criticised, either for being too general or too detailed. Some have argued, for example, that they do not go far enough in ensuring that MNEs comply with national law and practice, while others have said the Guidelines go beyond those standards in some areas. Another area of debate involves the follow-up, which some say needs to be made stronger, but which others argue is too juridical.

The decade of the 1990s poses new challenges for the Guidelines. Countries' and companies' roles are undergoing transformation that will affect investment relations and have implications for the Guidelines and investment policy-makers.

For companies, this transformation involves a complex web of relationships, alliances and agreements with other companies to establish and expand activities in foreign markets, spread costs, improve research and development capacities, and gain access to distribution networks. The rapid diffusion of technology means companies cannot maintain their technological advantage for long and must rely on others -- sometimes their competitors -- to benefit from technologies they cannot develop themselves. And the convergence of consumer preferences means customers world-wide demand the best products at the cheapest price, regardless of national origin. This leads to new ways of doing business in foreign markets.

For countries, the changes affect their role as homes or hosts to MNEs. Countries which before were mainly recipients of foreign direct investment and which favoured strict standards for MNEs now have their own companies investing abroad. Whereas these countries may have favoured strict standards for MNEs, they are now likely to take a more balanced view. Conversely, countries which before were predominantly capital-exporters and which may have supported a more flexible approach towards multinational enterprises now have numerous foreign enterprises in their own territories. This may lead them to look more closely at how the Guidelines apply to those foreign companies.

These changes suggest the Guidelines will continue to play a role in international economic co-operation in the 1990s. As countries evolve from being a home to host of MNEs, and vice-versa, the Guidelines can help maintain a balance between what MNEs can contribute to social and economic progress in those countries and what they can gain by investing there.

The Guidelines also provide a balanced framework within which companies can maximise commercial advantage while maintaining internationally accepted standards of corporate behaviour. This is particularly important as the competition for direct investment increases world-wide. Companies adhering to the Guidelines can be reasonably certain that they will seen by governments and trade unions as good corporate citizens, and will be able to carry out their operations in foreign markets on the basis of mutual confidence.

Annex 1

DECLARATION ON INTERNATIONAL INVESTMENT
AND MULTINATIONAL ENTERPRISES

(21 June 1976)

THE GOVERNMENTS OF OECD MEMBER COUNTRIES[1]

CONSIDERING:

-- That international investment has assumed increased importance in the world economy and has considerably contributed to the development of their countries;

-- That multinational enterprises play an important role in this investment process;

-- That co-operation by Member countries can improve the foreign investment climate, encourage the positive contribution which multinational enterprises can make to economic and social progress, and minimise and resolve difficulties which may arise from their various operations;

-- That, while continuing endeavours within the OECD may lead to further international arrangements and agreements in this field, it seems appropriate at this stage to intensify their co-operation and consultation on issue relating to international investment and multinational enterprises through inter-related instruments each of which deals with a different aspect of the matter and together constitute a framework within which the OECD will consider these issues;

DECLARE:

Guidelines for
Multinational
Enterprises

I. That they jointly recommend to multinational enterprises operating in their territories the observance of the Guidelines as set forth [below] having regard to the considerations and understandings which introduce the Guidelines and are an integral part of them;

National Treatment

II.1. That Member countries should, consistent with their needs to maintain public order, to protect their essential security interests and to fulfil commitments relating to international peace and security, accord to enterprises operating in their territories and owned or controlled directly or indirectly by nationals of another Member country (hereinafter referred to as "Foreign-Controlled Enterprises") treatment under their laws, regulations and administrative practices, consistent with international law and no less favourable than that accorded in like situations to domestic enterprises (hereinafter referred to as "National Treatment");

2. That Member countries will consider applying "National Treatment" in respect of countries other than Member countries;

3. That Member countries will endeavour to ensure that their territorial subdivisions apply "National Treatment";

4. That this Declaration does not deal with the right of Member countries to regulate the entry of foreign investment or the conditions of establishment of foreign enterprises;

Conflicting
Requirements

III. That they will co-operate with a view to avoiding or minimising the imposition of conflicting requirements on multinational enterprises and that they will take into account the general considerations and practical approaches as set forth in Annex 2 [to the Declaration].

International Investment Incentives and Disincentives	IV.1.	That they recognise the need to strengthen their co-operation in the field of international direct investment;
	2.	That they thus recognise the need to give due weight to the interests of Member countries affected by specific laws, regulations and administrative practices in this field (hereinafter called "measures") providing official incentives and disincentives to international direct investment;
	3.	That Member countries will endeavour to make such measures as transparent as possible, so that their importance and purpose can be ascertained and that information on them can be readily available;
Consultation Procedures	V.	That they are prepared to consult one another on the above matters in conformity with the Decisions of the Council on the Guidelines for Multinational Enterprises, on National Treatment and on International Investment Incentives and Disincentives;
Review	VI.	That they will review the above matters within three years with a view to improving the effectiveness of international economic co-operation among Member countries on issues relating to international investment and multinational enterprises[2].

GUIDELINES FOR MULTINATIONAL ENTERPRISES[3]

1.   Multinational enterprises now play an important part in the economies of Member countries and in international economic relations, which is of increasing interest to governments. Through international direct investment, such enterprises can bring substantial benefits to home and host countries by contributing to the efficient utilisation of capital, technology and human resources between countries and can thus fulfil an important role in the promotion of economic and social welfare. But the advances made by multinational enterprises in organising their operations beyond the national framework may lead to abuse of concentrations of economic power and to conflicts with national policy objectives. In addition, the

complexity of these multinational enterprises and the difficulty of clearly perceiving their diverse structures, operations and policies sometimes give rise to concern.

2.   The common aim of the Member countries is to encourage the positive contributions which multinational enterprises can make to economic and social progress and to minimise and resolve the difficulties to which their various operations may give rise.   In view of the transnational structure of such enterprises, this aim will be furthered by co-operation among the OECD countries where the headquarters of most of the multinational enterprises are established and which are the location of a substantial part of their operations.   The Guidelines set out hereafter are designed to assist in the achievement of this common aim and to contribute to improving the foreign investment climate.

3.   Since the operations of multinational enterprises extend throughout the world, including countries that are not Members of the Organisation, international co-operation in this field should extend to all States.   Member countries will give their full support to efforts undertaken in co-operation with non-member countries, and in particular with developing countries, with a view to improving the welfare and living standards of all people both by encouraging the positive contributions which multinational enterprises can make and by minimising and resolving the problems which may arise in connection with their activities.

4.   Within the Organisation, the programme of co-operation to attain these ends will be a continuing, pragmatic and balanced one.   It comes within the general aims of the Convention on the Organisation for Economic Co-operation and Development (OECD) and makes full use of the various specialised bodies of the Organisation, whose terms of reference already cover many aspects of the role of multinational enterprises, notably in matters of international trade and payments, competition, taxation, manpower, industrial development, science and technology. In these bodies, work is being carried out on the identification of issues, the improvement of relevant qualitative and statistical information and the elaboration of proposals for action designed to strengthen inter-governmental co-operation. In some of these areas procedures already exist through which issues related to the operations of multinational enterprises can be taken up.   This work could result in the conclusion of further and complementary agreements and arrangements between governments.

5.   The initial phase of the co-operation programme is composed of a Declaration and three Decisions promulgated simultaneously as they are complementary and inter-connected, in respect of Guidelines for multinational enterprises, National Treatment for foreign-controlled enterprises and international investment incentives and disincentives.

6.   The Guidelines set out below are recommendations jointly addressed by Member countries to multinational enterprises operating in their territories. These Guidelines, which take into account the problems which can arise because of the

international structure of these enterprises, lay down standards for the activities of these enterprises in the different Member countries. Observance of the Guidelines is voluntary and not legally enforceable. However, they should help to ensure that the operations of these enterprises are in harmony with national policies of the countries where they operate and to strengthen the basis of mutual confidence between enterprises and States.

7.   Every State has the right to prescribe the conditions under which multinational enterprises operate within its national jurisdiction, subject to international law and to the international agreements to which it has subscribed. The entities of a multinational enterprise located in various countries are subject to the laws of these countries.

8.   A precise legal definition of multinational enterprises is not required for the purposes of the Guidelines. These usually comprise companies or other entities whose ownership is private, state or mixed, established in different countries and so linked that one or more of them may be able to exercise a significant influence over the activities of others and, in particular, to share knowledge and resources with the others. The degrees of autonomy of each entity in relation to the others varies widely from one multinational enterprise to another, depending on the nature of the links between such entities and the fields of activity concerned. For these reasons, the Guidelines are addressed to the various entities within the multinational enterprise (parent companies and/or local entities) according to the actual distribution of responsibilities among them on the understanding that they will co-operate and provide assistance to one another as necessary to facilitate observance of the Guidelines. The word "enterprise" as used in these Guidelines refers to these various entities in accordance with their responsibilities.

9.   The Guidelines are not aimed at introducing differences of treatment between multinational and domestic enterprises; wherever relevant they reflect good practice for all. Accordingly, multinational and domestic enterprises are subject to the same expectations in respect of their conduct wherever the Guidelines are relevant to both.

10.   The use of appropriate international dispute settlement mechanisms, including arbitration, should be encouraged as a means of facilitating the resolution of problems arising between enterprises and Member countries.

11.   Member countries have agreed to establish appropriate review and consultation procedures concerning issues arising in respect of the Guidelines. When multinational enterprises are made subject to conflicting requirements by Member countries, the governments concerned will co-operate in good faith with a view to resolving such problems either within the Committee on International Investment and Multinational Enterprises established by the OECD Council on 21 January 1975 or through other mutually acceptable arrangements.

Having regard to the foregoing considerations, the Member countries set forth the following Guidelines for multinational enterprises with the understanding that Member countries will fulfil their responsibilities to treat enterprises equitably and in accordance with international law and international agreements as well as contractual obligations to which they have subscribed.

GENERAL POLICIES

Enterprises should:

1. Take fully into account established general policy objectives of the Member countries in which they operate;

2. In particular, give due consideration to those countries' aims and priorities with regard to economic and social progress, including industrial and regional development, the protection of the environment and consumer interests, the creation of employment opportunities, the promotion of innovation and the transfer of technology[4];

3. While observing their legal obligations concerning information, supply their entities with supplementary information the latter may need in order to meet requests by the authorities of the countries in which those entities are located for information relevant to the activities of those entities, taking into account legitimate requirements of business confidentiality;

4. Favour close co-operation with the local community and business interests;

5. Allow their component entities freedom to develop their activities and to exploit their competitive advantage in domestic and foreign markets, consistent with the need for specialisation and sound commercial practice;

6. When filling responsible posts in each country of operation, take due account of individual qualifications without discrimination as to nationality, subject to particular national requirements in this respect;

7. Not render and they should not be solicited or expected to render any bribe or other improper benefit, direct or indirect, to any public servant or holder of public office;

8. Unless legally permissible, not make contributions to candidates for public office or to political parties or other political organisations;

9. Abstain from any improper involvement in local political activities.

DISCLOSURE OF INFORMATION

Enterprises should, having due regard to their nature and relative size in the economic context of their operations and to requirements of business confidentiality and to cost, publish in a form suited to improve public understanding a sufficient body of factual information on the structure, activities and policies of the enterprise as a whole, as a supplement, in so far as necessary for this purpose, to information to be disclosed under the supplement, in so far as necessary for this purpose, to information to be disclosed under the national law of the individual countries in which they operate. To this end, they should publish within reasonable time limits, on a regular basis, but at least annually, financial statements and other pertinent information relating to the enterprise as a whole, comprising in particular:

a) The structure of the enterprise, showing the name and location of the parent company, its main affiliates, its percentage ownership, direct and indirect, in these affiliates, including shareholdings between them;

b) The geographical areas[5] where operations are carried out and the principal activities carried on therein by the parent company and the main affiliates;

c) The operating results and sales by geographical area and the sales in the major line of business for the enterprise as a whole;

d) Significant new capital investment by geographical area and, as far as practicable, by major lines of business for the enterprise as a whole;

e) A statement of the sources and uses of funds by the enterprise as a whole;

f) The average number of employees in each geographical area;

g) Research and development expenditure for the enterprise as a whole;

h) The policies followed in respect of intra-group pricing;

i) The accounting policies, including those on consolidation, observed in compiling the published information.

COMPETITION

Enterprises should, while conforming to official competition rules and established policies of the countries in which they operate:

1. Refrain from actions which would adversely affect competition in the relevant market by abusing a dominant position of market power, by means of, for example:

    a) Anti-competitive acquisitions;

    b) Predatory behaviour toward competitors;

    c) Unreasonable refusal to deal;

    d) Anti-competitive abuse of industrial property rights;

    e) Discriminatory (i.e. unreasonably differentiated) pricing and using such pricing transactions between affiliated enterprises as a means of affecting adversely competition outside these enterprises;

2. Allow purchasers, distributors and licensees freedom to resell, export, purchase and develop their operations consistent with law, trade conditions, the need for specialisation and sound commercial practice;

3. Refrain from participating in or otherwise purposely strengthening the restrictive effects of international or domestic cartels or restrictive agreements which adversely affect or eliminate competition and which are not generally or specifically accepted under applicable national or international legislation;

4. Be ready to consult and co-operate, including the provision of information, with competent authorities of countries whose interests are directly affected in regard to competition issues or investigations. Provisions of information should be in accordance with safeguards normally applicable in this field.

FINANCING

Enterprises should, in managing the financial and commercial operations of their activities, and especially their liquid foreign assets and liabilities, take into consideration the established objectives of the countries in which they operate regarding balance of payments and credit policies.

TAXATION

Enterprises should:

1. Upon request of the taxation authorities of the countries in which they operate provide, in accordance with the safeguards and relevant procedures of the national laws of these countries, the information necessary to determine correctly the taxes to be assessed in connection with their operations, including relevant information concerning their operations in other countries;

2. Refrain from making use of the particular facilities available to them, such as transfer pricing which does not conform to an arm's length standard, for modifying in ways contrary to national laws the tax base on which members of the group are assessed.

EMPLOYMENT AND INDUSTRIAL RELATIONS

Enterprises should, within the framework of law, regulations and prevailing labour relations and employment practices, in each of the countries in which they operate:

1. Respect the right of their employees to be represented by trade unions and other bona fide organisations of employees, and engage in constructive negotiations, either individually or through employers' associations, with such employee organisations with a view to reaching agreements on employment conditions, which should include provisions for dealing with disputes arising over the interpretation of such agreements, and for ensuring mutually respected rights and responsibilities;

2. a) Provide such facilities to representatives of the employees as may be necessary to assist in the development of effective collective agreements;

   b) Provide to representatives of employees information which is needed for meaningful negotiations on conditions of employment;

3. Provide to representatives of employees where this accords with local law and practice, information which enables them to obtain a true and fair view of the performance of the entity or, where appropriate, the enterprise as a whole;

4. Observe standards of employment and industrial relations not less favourable than those observed by comparable employers in the host country;

5. In their operations, to the greatest extent practicable, utilise, train and prepare for upgrading members of the local labour force in co-operation with representatives of their employees and, where appropriate, the relevant governmental authorities;

6. In considering changes in their operations which would have major effects upon the livelihood of their employees, in particular in the case of the closure of an entity involving collective lay-offs or dismissals, provide reasonable notice of such changes to representatives of their employees, and where appropriate to the relevant governmental authorities and co-operate with the employee representatives and appropriate governmental authorities so as to mitigate to the maximum extent practicable adverse effects;

7. Implement their employment policies including hiring, discharge, pay, promotion and training without discrimination unless selectivity in respect of employee characteristics is in furtherance of established governmental policies which specifically promote greater equality of employment opportunity;

8. In the context of bona fide negotiations[6] with representatives of employees on conditions of employment, or while employees are exercising a right to organise, not threaten to utilise a capacity to transfer the whole or part of an operating unit from the country concerned nor transfer employees from the enterprises' component entities in other countries in order to influence unfairly those negotiations or to hinder the exercise of a right to organise;[7]

9. Enable authorised representatives of their employees to conduct negotiations on collective bargaining or labour management relations issues with representatives of management who are authorised to take decisions on the matters under negotiation.

ENVIRONMENTAL PROTECTION[8]

Enterprises should, within the framework of laws, regulations and administrative practices in the countries in which they operate, and recalling the provisions of paragraph 9 of the Introduction to the Guidelines that, *inter alia*, multinational and domestic enterprises are subject to the same expectations in respect of their conduct whenever the Guidelines are relevant to both, take due account of the need to protect the environment and avoid creating environmentally related health problems. In particular, enterprises, whether multinational or domestic, should:

1. Assess, and take into account in decision making, foreseeable environmental and environmentally related health consequences of their activities, including siting decisions, impact on indigenous natural resources and foreseeable environmental and environmentally related health risks of products as well as from the generation, transport and disposal of waste;

2. Co-operate with competent authorities, inter alia, by providing adequate and timely information regarding the potential impacts on the environment and environmentally related health aspects of all their activities and by providing the relevant expertise available in the enterprise as a whole;

3. Take appropriate measures in their operations to minimise the risk of accidents and damage to health and the environment, and to co-operate in mitigating adverse effects, in particular:

   a) by selecting and adopting those technologies and practices which are compatible with these objectives;

   b) by introducing a system of environmental protection at the level of the enterprise as a whole including, where appropriate, the use of environmental auditing;

   c) by enabling their component entities to be adequately equipped, especially by providing them with adequate knowledge and assistance;

   d) by implementing education and training programmes for their employees;

   e) by preparing contingency plans; and

   f) by supporting, in an appropriate manner, public information and community awareness programmes.

SCIENCE AND TECHNOLOGY

Enterprises should:

1. Endeavour to ensure that their activities fit satisfactorily into the scientific and technological policies and plans of the countries in which they operate, and contribute to the development of national scientific and technological capacities, including as far as appropriate the establishment and improvement in host countries of their capacity to innovate;

2. To the fullest extent practicable, adopt in the course of their business activities practices which permit the rapid diffusion of technologies with due regard to the protection of industrial and intellectual property rights;

3. When granting licenses for the use of industrial property rights or when otherwise transferring technology, do so on reasonable terms and conditions.

Notes and References

1. On matters falling within its competence, the European Economic Community is associated with the section on National Treatment.

2. The Declaration was reviewed in 1979, 1984 and 1991. Section III on Conflicting Requirements was added following the 1991 Review.

3. The Guidelines were reviewed in 1979, 1984 and 1991. These reviews resulted in modification of the General Policies chapter (paragraph 2); the Disclosure of Information chapter [sub-paragraph *b*]; a clarification and modification of the Employment and Industrial Relations chapter (paragraph 8); and the addition of a new chapter on the Environment.

4. This paragraph includes the additional provision concerning consumer interests, adopted by the OECD Governments at the meeting of the OECD Council at Ministerial level on 17 and 18 May 1984.

*5. *For the purposes of the Guideline on Disclosure of Information, the term "geographical area" means groups of countries or individual countries as each enterprise determines is appropriate in its particular circumstances. While no single method of grouping is appropriate for all enterprises or for all purposes, the factors to be considered by an enterprise would include the significance of geographic proximity, economic affinity, similarities in business environments and the nature, scale and degree of interrelationship of the enterprises' operations in the various countries.*

*6. Bona fide negotiations may include labour disputes as part of the process of negotiation. Whether or not labour disputes are so included will be determined by the law and prevailing employment practices of particular countries.

7. This paragraph includes the additional provision, concerning transfer of employees, adopted by OECD Governments at the meeting of the OECD Council at Ministerial level on 13 and 14 June 1979.

8. This chapter was added at the meeting of the OECD Council at Ministerial level on 4 and 5 June 1991.

---

* These texts are integral parts of the negotiated instruments.

Annex 2

THE GUIDELINES FOR MULTINATIONAL ENTERPRISES:
SECOND REVISED DECISION OF THE COUNCIL

Amended June 1991

THE COUNCIL,

Having regard to the Convention on the Organisation for Economic Co-operation and Development of 14th December 1960 and, in particular, to Articles 2*d)*, 3 and 5*a)* thereof;

Having regard to the Resolution of the Council of 28th November 1979, on the Terms of Reference of the Committee on International Investment and Multinational Enterprises and, in particular, to paragraph 2 thereof [C(79)210(Final)];

Taking note of the Declaration by the Governments of OECD Member countries of 21st June 1976 in which they jointly recommend to multinational enterprises the observance of Guidelines for multinational enterprises;

Having regard to the Revised Decision of the Council of 13th June 1979 on Inter-Governmental Consultation Procedures on the Guidelines for Multinational Enterprises [C(79)143(Final)];

Recognising the desirability of setting forth procedures by which consultations may take place on matters related to these Guidelines;

Recognising that, while bilateral and multilateral co-operation should be strengthened when multinational enterprises are made subject to conflicting requirements, effective co-operation on problems arising therefrom may best be pursued in most circumstances on a bilateral level, although there may be cases where the multilateral approach would be more effective;

71

Considering the Report on the Review of the 1976 Declaration and Decisions on International Investment and Multinational Enterprises [C(79)102(Final)] and the Report on the Second Review of the 1976 Declaration and Decisions on International Investment and Multinational Enterprises [C/MIN(84)5(Final)], including the particular endorsement of the section in the Second Review Report relating to conflicting requirements;

On the proposal of the Committee on International Investment and Multinational Enterprises:

DECIDES:

1.   Member Governments shall set up National Contact Points for undertaking promotional activities, handling inquires and for discussions with the parties concerned on all matters related to the Guidelines so that they can contribute to the solution of problems which may arise in this connection. The business community, employee organisations and other interested parties shall be informed of the availability of such facilities.

2.   National Contact Points in different countries shall co-operate if such need arises, on any matter related to the Guidelines relevant to their activities. As a general procedure, discussions at the national level should be initiated before contacts with other National Contact Points are undertaken.

3.   The Committee on International Investment and Multinational Enterprises (hereinafter called "the Committee") shall periodically or at the request of a Member country hold an exchange of views on matters related to the Guidelines and the experience gained in their application. The Committee shall be responsible for clarification of the Guidelines. Clarification will be provided as required. The Committee shall periodically report to the Council on these matters.

4.   The Committee shall periodically invite the Business and Industry Advisory Committee to OECD (BIAC) and the Trade Union Advisory Committee to OECD (TUAC) to express their views on matters related to the Guidelines. In addition, exchanges of views with the advisory bodies on these matters may be held upon request by the latter. The Committee shall take account of such views in its reports to the Council.

5.   If it so wishes, an individual enterprise will be given the opportunity to express its views either orally or in writing on issues concerning the Guidelines involving its interests.

6.   The Committee shall not reach conclusions on the conduct of individual enterprises.

7. This Decision shall be reviewed at the latest in six years. The Committee shall make proposals for this purpose as appropriate.

8. This Decision shall replace Decision [C(79)143].

NATIONAL CONTACT POINTS

AUSTRALIA

Executive Member
Foreign Investment Review Board
C/- The Treasury
Parkes Place
Parkes Act 2600
Canberra

Phone: (61) 62 63 3795
Fax: (61) 62 63 2940

AUSTRIA

Director
Ministry for Economic Affairs
Division IV/1
Stubenring 1
1011 Vienna

Phone: (43) 222 71100 5234
Fax: (43) 222 7142719 or 7137995

BELGIUM

Directeur général honoraire
Ministère des Affaires Economiques
Rue du Cornet 43
1040 Bruxelles

Phone: (32) 2 230 90 43
Fax: (32) 2 230 00 50

CANADA	Deputy Director Investment Group Trade Competitiveness Policy Division External Affairs and International Trade Canada Tower C-6 125 Sussex Drive Ottawa, Ontario K1A 0G2

Phone: (1) 613 995 8224 or 992 0484
Fax: (1) 613 944 0679 or 992 6002

DENMARK	Head of Section Ministry of Industry Slotsholmsgade 12 DK-1216 Copenhagen K

Phone: (45) 33 923 350
Fax: (45) 33 123 778

FINLAND	Industrial Counsellor Industrial Department Ministry of Trade and Industry Aleksi 4 FIN-00170 Helsinki

Phone: (358) 0 160 3603
Fax: (358) 0 160 2694

FRANCE	Chef de Bureau Ministère de l'économie et des finances Direction du trésor Service des affaires internationales Sous-Direction des affaires multilatérales Télédoc 579 139, rue de Bercy 75572 Paris Cedex 12

Phone: (33) 1 44 87 73 72
Fax: (33) 1 40 04 29 25

GERMANY	Head of Department Federal Ministry of Economics Section V C 5 Bundeswirtschaftsministerium Villemombler Str. 76 Postfach 14 02 60 5300 Bonn Phone: (49) 228 615 3758 Fax: (49) 228 615 2332
GREECE	Director Directorate for International Economic Organizations Ministry of National Economy Nikis 3 10180 Athens Phone: (30) 1 333 2121 Fax: (30) 1 323 4430
ICELAND	Director for Financial Markets and Economic Affairs Ministry of Industry and Commerce Arnarhvoli 150 Reykjavik Phone: (354) 1 609 070 Fax: (354) 1 621 289
IRELAND	Department of Enterprise and Employment Kildare Street Dublin 2 Phone: (353) 1 661 4444 Fax: (353) 1 676 2654

ITALY	Secrétariat Général de la Programmation Economique Ministère du Budget et de la Programmation Economique Via XX Settembre 00187 Roma
	Phone: (39) 6 47611 - 47.61.30.99 Fax: (39) 6 48.36.44
JAPAN	Director Second International Organisation Division Ministry of Foreign Affairs 2-2-1 Kasumigaseki Chiyoda-ku Tokyo
	Phone: (81) 3 3580 3311 Fax: (81) 3 3503 3136
LUXEMBOURG	Ministry of Economics 19-21 Boulevard Royal
	Treasury Ministry 3, rue de la Congrégation
	Tel: (352) 47 81 Fax: (352) 46 62 12
NETHERLANDS	Head of the International Investment Division Directorate-General for Foreign Economic Relations Ministry of Economic Affairs P.O. Box 20101 2500 EC The Hague
	Phone: (31) 70 379 7152 Fax: (31) 70 379 8808

NEW ZEALAND	OECD Liaison Officer Ministry of Foreign Affairs and Trade Private Bag Wellington
	Phone: (64) 4 472 8877 Fax: (64) 4 472 9596
NORWAY	Ministry of Foreign Affairs Department of External Economic Affairs II, OECD-section P.O. Box 8114 Dep. 0032 Oslo
	Phone: (47) 22 34 36 00 Fax: (47) 22 34 95 80
PORTUGAL	Director Foreign Investment Department ICEP - Investments, Trade and Tourism of Portugal Avenida 5 de Outubro, 101 1000 Lisboa
	Phone: (351) 1 793 0103 Fax: (351) 1 795 2329
SPAIN	Deputy Director Spanish Investment Abroad General Directorate of External Investment Ministry of Industry, Trade and Tourism Paseo de la Castellana, 162 - Floor 13 28071 Madrid
	Phone: (34) 1 349 36 19 Fax: (34) 1 349 35 62

SWEDEN	Head of Section Working Group on Multinational Enterprises Ministry of Industry and Commerce 103 33 Stockholm
	Phone: (46) 8 763 2204 or 763 1000 Fax: (46) 8 113616
SWITZERLAND	Service des investissements internationaux Office fédéral des affaires économiques extérieures Département fédéral de l'économie publique Palais fédéral est, 3003 Berne
	Phone: (41) 31 61 22 91 Fax: (41) 31 21 53 72
TURKEY	Undersecretariat of Treasury and Foreign Trade General Directorate of Foreign Investment Inönü Bulvari Emek - Ankara
	Phone: (90) 4 212 58 80 Fax: (90) 4 212 89 16
UNITED KINGDOM	Department of Trade and Industry International Trade Policy Division Ashdown House 123 Victoria Street London SW1E 6RB
	Phone: (44) 71 215 6147 Fax: (44) 71 215 6767

UNITED STATES

Director
Office of Investment Affairs
Room 2533A
US Department of State
2201 C St. NW
Washington, DC 20520

Phone: (1) 202 647 4416 or 647 2726
Fax: (1) 202 647 0320

MAIN SALES OUTLETS OF OECD PUBLICATIONS
PRINCIPAUX POINTS DE VENTE DES PUBLICATIONS DE L'OCDE

ARGENTINA – ARGENTINE
Carlos Hirsch S.R.L.
Galería Güemes, Florida 165, 4° Piso
1333 Buenos Aires   Tel. (1) 331.1787 y 331.2391
Telefax: (1) 331.1787

AUSTRALIA – AUSTRALIE
D.A. Information Services
648 Whitehorse Road, P.O.B 163
Mitcham, Victoria 3132   Tel. (03) 873.4411
Telefax: (03) 873.5679

AUSTRIA – AUTRICHE
Gerold & Co.
Graben 31
Wien I   Tel. (0222) 533.50.14

BELGIUM – BELGIQUE
Jean De Lannoy
Avenue du Roi 202
B-1060 Bruxelles   Tel. (02) 538.51.69/538.08.41
Telefax: (02) 538.08.41

CANADA
Renouf Publishing Company Ltd.
1294 Algoma Road
Ottawa, ON K1B 3W8   Tel. (613) 741.4333
Telefax: (613) 741.5439
Stores:
61 Sparks Street
Ottawa, ON K1P 5R1   Tel. (613) 238.8985
211 Yonge Street
Toronto, ON M5B 1M4   Tel. (416) 363.3171
Telefax: (416)363.59.63
Les Éditions La Liberté Inc.
3020 Chemin Sainte-Foy
Sainte-Foy, PQ G1X 3V6   Tel. (418) 658.3763
Telefax: (418) 658.3763

Federal Publications Inc.
165 University Avenue, Suite 701
Toronto, ON M5H 3B8   Tel. (416) 860.1611
Telefax: (416) 860.1608
Les Publications Fédérales
1185 Université
Montréal, QC H3B 3A7   Tel. (514) 954.1633
Telefax : (514) 954.1635

CHINA – CHINE
China National Publications Import
Export Corporation (CNPIEC)
16 Gongti E. Road, Chaoyang District
P.O. Box 88 or 50
Beijing 100704 PR   Tel. (01) 506.6688
Telefax; (01) 506.3101

DENMARK – DANEMARK
Munksgaard Book and Subscription Service
35, Nørre Søgade, P.O. Box 2148
DK-1016 København K   Tel. (33) 12.85.70
Telefax: (33) 12.93.87

FINLAND – FINLANDE
Akateeminen Kirjakauppa
Keskuskatu 1, P.O. Box 128
00100 Helsinki
Subscription Services/Agence d'abonnements :
P.O. Box 23
00371 Helsinki   Tel. (358 0) 12141
Telefax: (358 0) 121.4450

FRANCE
OECD/OCDE
Mail Orders/Commandes par correspondance:
2, rue André-Pascal
75775 Paris Cedex 16   Tel. (33-1) 45.24.82.00
Telefax: (33-1) 45.24.81.76   or (33-1) 45.24.85.00
Telex: 640048 OCDE

OECD Bookshop/Librairie de l'OCDE :
33, rue Octave-Feuillet
75016 Paris   Tel. (33-1) 45.24.81.67
(33-1) 45.24.81.81
Documentation Française
29, quai Voltaire
75007 Paris   Tel. 40.15.70.00
Gibert Jeune (Droit-Économie)
6, place Saint-Michel
75006 Paris   Tel. 43.25.91.19
Librairie du Commerce International
10, avenue d'Iéna
75016 Paris   Tel. 40.73.34.60
Librairie Dunod
Université Paris-Dauphine
Place du Maréchal de Lattre de Tassigny
75016 Paris   Tel. (1) 44.05.40.13
Librairie Lavoisier
11, rue Lavoisier
75008 Paris   Tel. 42.65.39.95
Librairie L.G.D.J. - Montchrestien
20, rue Soufflot
75005 Paris   Tel. 46.33.89.85
Librairie des Sciences Politiques
30, rue Saint-Guillaume
75007 Paris   Tel. 45.48.36.02
P.U.F.
49, boulevard Saint-Michel
75005 Paris   Tel. 43.25.83.40
Librairie de l'Université
12a, rue Nazareth
13100 Aix-en-Provence   Tel. (16) 42.26.18.08
Documentation Française
165, rue Garibaldi
69003 Lyon   Tel. (16) 78.63.32.23
Librairie Decitre
29, place Bellecour
69002 Lyon   Tel. (16) 72.40.54.54

GERMANY – ALLEMAGNE
OECD Publications and Information Centre
August-Bebel-Allee 6
D-53175 Bonn 2   Tel. (0228) 959.120
Telefax: (0228) 959.12.17

GREECE – GRÈCE
Librairie Kauffmann
Mavrokordatou 9
106 78 Athens   Tel. (01) 32.55.321
Telefax: (01) 36.33.967

HONG-KONG
Swindon Book Co. Ltd.
13–15 Lock Road
Kowloon, Hong Kong   Tel. 366.80.31
Telefax: 739.49.75

HUNGARY – HONGRIE
Euro Info Service
POB 1271
1464 Budapest   Tel. (1) 111.62.16
Telefax : (1) 111.60.61

ICELAND – ISLANDE
Mál Mog Menning
Laugavegi 18, Pósthólf 392
121 Reykjavik   Tel. 162.35.23

INDIA – INDE
Oxford Book and Stationery Co.
Scindia House
New Delhi 110001   Tel.(11) 331.5896/5308
Telefax: (11) 332.5993
17 Park Street
Calcutta 700016   Tel. 240832

INDONESIA – INDONÉSIE
Pdii-Lipi
P.O. Box 269/JKSMG/88
Jakarta 12790   Tel. 583467
Telex: 62 875

IRELAND – IRLANDE
TDC Publishers – Library Suppliers
12 North Frederick Street
Dublin 1   Tel. (01) 874.48.35
Telefax: (01) 874.84.16

ISRAEL
Electronic Publications only
Publications électroniques seulement
Sophist Systems Ltd.
71 Allenby Street
Tel-Aviv 65134   Tel. 3-29.00.21
Telefax: 3-29.92.39

ITALY – ITALIE
Libreria Commissionaria Sansoni
Via Duca di Calabria 1/1
50125 Firenze   Tel. (055) 64.54.15
Telefax: (055) 64.12.57
Via Bartolini 29
20155 Milano   Tel. (02) 36.50.83
Editrice e Libreria Herder
Piazza Montecitorio 120
00186 Roma   Tel. 679.46.28
Telefax: 678.47.51
Libreria Hoepli
Via Hoepli 5
20121 Milano   Tel. (02) 86.54.46
Telefax: (02) 805.28.86
Libreria Scientifica
Dott. Lucio de Biasio 'Aeiou'
Via Coronelli, 6
20146 Milano   Tel. (02) 48.95.45.52
Telefax: (02) 48.95.45.48

JAPAN – JAPON
OECD Publications and Information Centre
Landic Akasaka Building
2-3-4 Akasaka, Minato-ku
Tokyo 107   Tel. (81.3) 3586.2016
Telefax: (81.3) 3584.7929

KOREA – CORÉE
Kyobo Book Centre Co. Ltd.
P.O. Box 1658, Kwang Hwa Moon
Seoul   Tel. 730.78.91
Telefax: 735.00.30

MALAYSIA – MALAISIE
Co-operative Bookshop Ltd.
University of Malaya
P.O. Box 1127, Jalan Pantai Baru
59700 Kuala Lumpur
Malaysia   Tel. 756.5000/756.5425
Telefax: 757.3661

MEXICO – MEXIQUE
Revistas y Periodicos Internacionales S.A. de C.V.
Florencia 57 - 1004
Mexico, D.F. 06600   Tel. 207.81.00
Telefax : 208.39.79

NETHERLANDS – PAYS-BAS
SDU Uitgeverij Plantijnstraat
Externe Fondsen
Postbus 20014
2500 EA's-Gravenhage   Tel. (070) 37.89.880
Voor bestellingen: Telefax: (070) 34.75.778

NEW ZEALAND
NOUVELLE-ZÉLANDE
Legislation Services
P.O. Box 12418
Thorndon, Wellington   Tel. (04) 496.5652
                              Telefax: (04) 496.5698

NORWAY – NORVÈGE
Narvesen Info Center – NIC
Bertrand Narvesens vei 2
P.O. Box 6125 Etterstad
0602 Oslo 6   Tel. (022) 57.33.00
                             Telefax: (022) 68.19.01

PAKISTAN
Mirza Book Agency
65 Shahrah Quaid-E-Azam
Lahore 54000   Tel. (42) 353.601
                             Telefax: (42) 231.730

PHILIPPINE – PHILIPPINES
International Book Center
5th Floor, Filipinas Life Bldg.
Ayala Avenue
Metro Manila   Tel. 81.96.76
                      Telex 23312 RHP PH

PORTUGAL
Livraria Portugal
Rua do Carmo 70-74
Apart. 2681
1200 Lisboa   Tel.: (01) 347.49.82/5
                            Telefax: (01) 347.02.64

SINGAPORE – SINGAPOUR
Gower Asia Pacific Pte Ltd.
Golden Wheel Building
41, Kallang Pudding Road, No. 04-03
Singapore 1334   Tel. 741.5166
                             Telefax: 742.9356

SPAIN – ESPAGNE
Mundi-Prensa Libros S.A.
Castelló 37, Apartado 1223
Madrid 28001   Tel. (91) 431.33.99
                             Telefax: (91) 575.39.98

Librería Internacional AEDOS
Consejo de Ciento 391
08009 – Barcelona   Tel. (93) 488.30.09
                             Telefax: (93) 487.76.59
Llibreria de la Generalitat
Palau Moja
Rambla dels Estudis, 118
08002 – Barcelona
          (Subscripcions) Tel. (93) 318.80.12
          (Publicacions) Tel. (93) 302.67.23
                             Telefax: (93) 412.18.54

SRI LANKA
Centre for Policy Research
c/o Colombo Agencies Ltd.
No. 300-304, Galle Road
Colombo 3   Tel. (1) 574240, 573551-2
                  Telefax: (1) 575394, 510711

SWEDEN – SUÈDE
Fritzes Information Center
Box 16356
Regeringsgatan 12
106 47 Stockholm   Tel. (08) 690.90.90
                             Telefax: (08) 20.50.21

Subscription Agency/Agence d'abonnements :
Wennergren-Williams Info AB
P.O. Box 1305
171 25 Solna   Tel. (08) 705.97.50
                            Téléfax : (08) 27.00.71

SWITZERLAND – SUISSE
Maditec S.A. (Books and Periodicals - Livres
et périodiques)
Chemin des Palettes 4
Case postale 266
1020 Renens   Tel. (021) 635.08.65
                            Telefax: (021) 635.07.80

Librairie Payot S.A.
4, place Pépinet
CP 3212
1002 Lausanne   Tel. (021) 341.33.48
                            Telefax: (021) 341.33.45

Librairie Unilivres
6, rue de Candolle
1205 Genève   Tel. (022) 320.26.23
                            Telefax: (022) 329.73.18

Subscription Agency/Agence d'abonnements :
Dynapresse Marketing S.A.
38 avenue Vibert
1227 Carouge   Tel.: (022) 308.07.89
                            Telefax : (022) 308.07.99

See also – Voir aussi :
OECD Publications and Information Centre
August-Bebel-Allee 6
D-53175 Bonn 2 (Germany)   Tel. (0228) 959.120
                            Telefax: (0228) 959.12.17

TAIWAN – FORMOSE
Good Faith Worldwide Int'l. Co. Ltd.
9th Floor, No. 118, Sec. 2
Chung Hsiao E. Road
Taipei   Tel. (02) 391.7396/391.7397
                            Telefax: (02) 394.9176

THAILAND – THAÏLANDE
Suksit Siam Co. Ltd.
113, 115 Fuang Nakhon Rd.
Opp. Wat Rajbopith
Bangkok 10200   Tel. (662) 225.9531/2
                            Telefax: (662) 222.5188

TURKEY – TURQUIE
Kültür Yayinlari Is-Türk Ltd. Sti.
Atatürk Bulvari No. 191/Kat 13
Kavaklidere/Ankara   Tel. 428.11.40 Ext. 2458
Dolmabahce Cad. No. 29
Besiktas/Istanbul   Tel. 260.71.88
                             Telex: 43482B

UNITED KINGDOM – ROYAUME-UNI
HMSO
Gen. enquiries   Tel. (071) 873 0011
Postal orders only:
P.O. Box 276, London SW8 5DT
Personal Callers HMSO Bookshop
49 High Holborn, London WC1V 6HB
                            Telefax: (071) 873 8200
Branches at: Belfast, Birmingham, Bristol, Edin-
burgh, Manchester

UNITED STATES – ÉTATS-UNIS
OECD Publications and Information Centre
2001 L Street N.W., Suite 700
Washington, D.C. 20036-4910 Tel. (202) 785.6323
                            Telefax: (202) 785.0350

VENEZUELA
Libreria del Este
Avda F. Miranda 52, Aptdo. 60337
Edificio Galipán
Caracas 106   Tel. 951.1705/951.2307/951.1297
                   Telegram: Libreste Caracas

Subscription to OECD periodicals may also be
placed through main subscription agencies.

Les abonnements aux publications périodiques de
l'OCDE peuvent être souscrits auprès des
principales agences d'abonnement.

Orders and inquiries from countries where Distributors have not yet been appointed should be sent to:
OECD Publications Service, 2 rue André-Pascal,
75775 Paris Cedex 16, France.

Les commandes provenant de pays où l'OCDE n'a
pas encore désigné de distributeur devraient être
adressées à : OCDE, Service des Publications,
2, rue André-Pascal, 75775 Paris Cedex 16, France.

2-1994

OECD PUBLICATIONS, 2 rue André-Pascal, 75775 PARIS CEDEX 16
PRINTED IN FRANCE
(21 94 02 1) ISBN 92-64-14109-X No. 47013 1994